D1760714

JOHN LE NEVE

Fasti Ecclesiae Anglicanae
1300–1541

Fasti Ecclesiae Anglicanae

1066–1300

1. St Paul's, London, comp. D. E. Greenway

2. Monastic Cathedrals (*Northern and Southern Provinces*), comp. D. E. Greenway

3. Lincoln, comp. D. E. Greenway

4. Salisbury, comp. D. E. Greenway

5. Chichester, comp. D. E. Greenway

6. York, comp. D. E. Greenway

7. Bath and Wells, comp. D. E. Greenway

8. Hereford, comp. J. S. Barrow

9. The Welsh Cathedrals, comp. M. J. Pearson

10. Exeter, comp. D. E. Greenway

The Personnel of the Norman Cathedrals during the Ducal Period, 911–1204, by D. S. Spear

1300–1541

First edition complete in 12 volumes (1962–5)

Second edition
Hereford Diocese, comp. J. M. Horn; rev. D. N. Lepine

1541–1857

1. St Paul's London, comp. J. M. Horn

2. Chichester Diocese, comp. J. M. Horn

3. Canterbury, Rochester and Winchester Dioceses, comp. J. M. Horn

4. York Diocese, comp. J. M. Horn and D. M. Smith

5. Bath and Wells Diocese, comp. J. M. Horn and D. S. Bailey

6. Salisbury Diocese, comp. J. M. Horn

7. Ely, Norwich, Westminster and Worcester Dioceses, comp. J. M. Horn

8. Bristol, Gloucester, Oxford and Peterborough Dioceses, comp. J. M. Horn

9. Lincoln Diocese, comp. J. M. Horn and D. M. Smith

10. Coventry and Lichfield Diocese, comp. J. M. Horn

11. Carlisle, Chester, Durham, Manchester, Ripon, and Sodor and Man Dioceses, comp. J. M. Horn, D. M. Smith and P. Mussett

12. Exeter Diocese, comp. W. H. Campbell

JOHN LE NEVE

Fasti Ecclesiae Anglicanae
1300–1541

II

Hereford Diocese

COMPILED BY
JOYCE M. HORN

REVISED BY
DAVID N. LEPINE

UNIVERSITY OF LONDON
SCHOOL OF ADVANCED STUDY
INSTITUTE OF HISTORICAL RESEARCH

2009

Published by
UNIVERSITY OF LONDON
SCHOOL OF ADVANCED STUDY
INSTITUTE OF HISTORICAL RESEARCH
Senate House, London, WC1E 7HU

© *University of London* 2009

ISBN - 978 1 905165 50 6

Typeset by Olwen Myhill

Printed in Great Britain by
Cromwell Press Group, Aintree Avenue, White Horse Business Park,
Trowbridge, Wilts BA14 0XB

Acknowledgements

My thanks go to my predecessors in this field, particularly to the pioneering work of Joyce Horn whose original edition forms the foundation of this revision. All scholars of Hereford cathedral owe a great deal to the work of Julia Barrow. Her edition of the 1066–1300 Fasti for Hereford is both authoritative and indispensable. I have relied heavily on it. Bill Campbell has been supportive, encouraging and generous. At Hereford the archivist Mrs. Rosalind Caird has not only been welcoming, efficient and resourceful but has saved me from error. My thanks also go to the Fasti Advisory Committee for their support and willingness to publish a revised version of the original edition.

David N. Lepine
2009

Contents

References

WORKS IN PRINT

The following abbreviations are used for works in print which are cited in the text three times or more. This is not an exhaustive list of works consulted. Unless otherwise stated, place of publication is London.

BRUC	A. B. Emden, *A Biographical Register of the University of Cambridge to 1500*. Cambridge, 1963.
BRUO	A. B. Emden, *A Biographical Register of the University of Oxford to A.D. 1500*. 3 vols. Oxford, 1957–9.
BRUO 1500–40	A. B. Emden, *A Biographical Register of the University of Oxford 1500–40*. Oxford, 1974.
CCR	*Calendar of the Close Rolls preserved in the Public Record Office*. 54 vols. 1892–1954.
Ch. & Rec.	*Charters and Records of Hereford Cathedral*, ed. W. W. Capes. Hereford, 1908.
CPL	*Calendar of Entries in the Papal Registers relating to Great Britain and Ireland: Papal Letters*. 18 vols. 1893–. In progress.
CPP	*Calendar of Entries in the Papal Registers relating to Great Britain and Ireland: Petitions to the Pope 1342–1419*. 1896.
CPR	*Calendar of the Patent Rolls preserved in the Public Record Office (1232–1509)*. 52 vols. 1891–1916.
Eubel	*Hierarchia Catholica Medii Aevi*, ed. C. Eubel. 3 vols. Münster, 1913–23.
Fasti Hereford 1066–1300	J. Le Neve, *Fasti Ecclesiae Anglicanae 1066–1300*, viii: *Hereford*, comp. J. Barrow. 2002.
Foedera	*Foedera, Conventiones, Literae et Cujuscunque Generis Acta Publica inter Reges Angliae et Alios Quosuis Imperatores ...*, ed. T. Rymer. 3rd edn. 10 vols. 1745.
Gallia Christiana	*Gallia Christiana*, ed. D. de Ste-Marthe and B. Hauréau. 16 vols. Paris, 1715–1865.
Havergal, *Mon. Inscr. Heref.*	F. T. Havergal, *Monumental Inscriptions in the Cathedral Church of Hereford*. Hereford, 1881.
Hemingby's Register	*Hemingby's Register*, ed. H. M. Chew. Wiltshire Record Society xviii, 1963.

L&G	*Accounts Rendered by Papal Collectors in England 1317–78*, ed. W. E. Lunt and E. B. Graves. Memoirs of the American Philosophical Society lxx, 1968.
L&P	*Letters and Papers of the Reign of Henry VIII*, ed. J. S. Brewer. 23 vols. in 38. 1862–1932.
Lettres Jean XXII	*Jean XXII: Lettres Communes*, ed. G. Mollat. 16 vols. Bibliothèque des Ecoles Françaises d'Athènes et de Rome, 3rd series i bis. Paris, 1904–47.
Lettres Benoît XII	*Benoît XII: Lettres Communes*, ed. J.-M. Vidal. 3 vols. Bibliothèque des Ecoles Françaises d'Athènes et de Rome, 3rd series i bis. Paris, 1903–11.
Lettres Urbain V	*Urbain V: Lettres Communes*, ed. M.-H. Laurent *et al.* 13 vols. Bibliothèque des Ecoles Françaises d'Athènes et de Rome, 3rd series i bis. Paris, 1954–89.
Lettres Grégoire XI	*Grégoire XI: Lettres Communes*, ed. A.-M. Hayes. Bibliothèque des Ecoles Françaises d'Athènes et de Rome, 3rd series i bis. Paris, 1992–. In progress.
LS	*Statutes of Lincoln Cathedral*, arranged H. Bradshaw, ed. C. Wordsworth. 2 vols. in 3. Cambridge, 1892–7.
McDermid, *Beverley Fasti*	R. T. W. McDermid, *Beverley Minster Fasti*. Yorkshire Archaeological Society Record Series cxlix, 1993.
ODNB	*Oxford Dictionary of National Biography*. Oxford 2004, online edn. 2007.
Reg. Beauchamp	*Registrum Ricardi Beauchamp, Episcopi Herefordensis 1449–50*, ed. A. T. Bannister. Canterbury and York Society xxv, 1919.
Reg. Booth	*Registrum Caroli Booth, Episcopi Herefordensis 1516–35*, ed. A. T. Bannister. Canterbury and York Society xxviii, 1921.
Reg. Boulers	*Registrum Reginaldi Boulers, Episcopi Herefordensis 1450–53*, ed. A. T. Bannister. Canterbury and York Society xxv, 1919.
Reg. Bransford	*A Calendar of the Register of Wolstan de Bransford, Bishop of Worcester 1339–1349*, ed. R. M. Haines. Worcestershire Historical Society, new series iv, 1966.
Reg. Brantingham	*The Register of Thomas Brantingham, Bishop of Exeter, 1370–94*, ed. F. C. Hingeston-Randolph. 1901–6.
Reg. Cantilupe	*Registrum Thome de Cantilupo, Episcopi Herefordensis AD MCCLXXV–MCCLXXXII*, ed. R. G. Griffiths and W. W. Capes. 2 vols. Canterbury and York Society ii, 1907.

Reg. L. Charlton	*Registrum Ludowici de Charltone, Episcopi Herefordensis 1361–70*, ed. J. H. Parry. Canterbury and York Society xiv, 1913.
Reg. T. Charlton	*Registrum Thome de Charltone, Episcopi Herefordensis 1327–44*, ed. W. W. Capes. Canterbury and York Society ix, 1913.
Reg. Chichele	*The Register of Henry Chichele, Archbishop of Canterbury, 1413–43*, ed. E. F. Jacobs. 4 vols. Canterbury and York Society xlii, xlv–xlvii, 1943–7.
Reg. Clement V	*Registrum Clementis Papae V*, ed. the Order of Saint Benedict. 8 vols. Rome, 1885–92.
Reg. Courtenay	*Registrum Willelmi de Courtenay, Episcopi Herefordensis 1370–5*, ed. W. W. Capes. Canterbury and York Society xv, 1914.
Reg. Gilbert	*Registrum Johannis Gilbert, Episcopi Herefordensis 1375–89*, ed. J. H. Parry. Canterbury and York Society xviii, 1915.
Reg. Innocent IV	*Les registres d'Innocent IV*, ed. E. Berger. Bibliothèque des Ecoles Françaises d'Athènes et de Rome, 2nd series i. Paris, 1884–1921.
Reg. Lacy Exeter	*The Register of Edmund Lacy, Bishop of Exeter 1420–1455: Part I, the Register of Institutions together with some Account of the Episcopate of John Catterik, 1419*, ed. F. C. Hingeston-Randolph. 1909.
Reg. Lacy H	*Registrum Edmundi Lacy, Episcopi Herefordensis 1417–20*, ed. J. H. Parry and A. T. Bannister. Canterbury and York Society xxii, 1918.
Reg. Langham	*Registrum Simonis de Langham, Cantuariensis archiepiscopi* [1366–8], ed. A. C. Wood. Canterbury and York Society lii, 1956.
Reg. Mascall	*Registrum Roberti Mascall, Episcopi Herefordensis 1404–16*, ed. J. H. Parry. Canterbury and York Society xxi, 1917.
Reg. Mayew	*Registrum Ricardi Mayew, Episcopi Herefordensis 1504–16*, ed. A. T. Bannister. Canterbury and York Society xxvii, 1921.
Reg. Myllyng	*Registrum Thome Myllyng, Episcopi Herefordensis 1474–92*, ed. A. T. Bannister. Canterbury and York Society xxvi, 1920.
Reg. Orleton	*Registrum Ade de Orleton, Episcopi Herefordensis A.D. MCCCXVII–MCCCXXVII*, ed. A. T. Bannister. Canterbury and York Society v, 1908.
Reg. Parker	*Registrum Matthei Parker, Diocesis Cantuariensis, A.D. 1559–75*, ed. E. M. Thompson and W. H. Frere. 1 vol. in 3. Canterbury and York Society xxv–xxvi, xxxix, 1928–33.

Reg. Polton   *Registrum Thome Polton, Episcopi Herefordensis 1420–22*, ed. W. W. Capes. Canterbury and York Society xxii, 1918.

Reg. Spofford   *Registrum Thomas Spofford, Episcopi Herefordensis, A.D. MCCCCXXII–MCCCCXLVIII*, ed. A. T. Bannister. Canterbury and York Society xxiii, 1919.

Reg. Sudbury   *Registrum Simonis de Sudbiria*, ed. R. C. Fowler and C. Jenkins. Canterbury and York Society, xxxviii, 1930.

Reg. Swinfield   *Registrum Ricardi de Swinfield, Episcopi Herefordensis, A.D. MCCLXXIII–MCCCXVII*, ed. W. W. Capes. Canterbury and York Society vi, 1909.

Reg. Trefnant   *Registrum Johannis Trefnant, Episcopi Herefordensis, MCCCIV–MCCCXVI*, ed. W. W. Capes. Canterbury and York Society xx, 1916.

Reg. Trillek   *Registrum Johannis de Trillek, Episcopi Herefordensis 1344–61*, ed. J. H. Parry. Canterbury and York Society viii, 1912.

Reg. Wykeham   *Wykeham's Register*, ed. T. F. Kirby. 2 vols. Hampshire Record Society, 1896–9.

Richardson, *Chancery*   M. Richardson, *The Medieval Chancery under Henry V*. List and Index Society Special Series xxx, 1999.

Survey of Cath.   *Survey of Cathedrals*, comp. B. Willis. 3 vols. in 2. 1742.

Taxatio   *Taxatio Ecclesiastica Angliae et Wallia auctoritate Nicolai IV*. Record Commission, 1802.

Thompson, *Lincoln Visitations*   *Visitations of Religious Houses in the Diocese of Lincoln*, ed. A. H. Thompson. 3 vols. Canterbury and York Society xvii, xxiv, xxxiii, 1915–27.

Valor   *Valor Ecclesiasticus temp. Henr. VIII*, ed. J. Caley and J. Hunter. 6 vols. in 4. Record Commission, 1810–34.

IN MANUSCRIPT

This list omits manuscripts from other repositories cited fewer than three times. These are cited in full when used.

Canterbury Cathedral Library
Registers of the Dean and Chapter: A, F, S and T

Lambeth Palace Library
Registers of the archbishops of Canterbury

Hereford Cathedral Archives

HCA 7031/1	Chapter Act Book 1512–66
HCA R2–120	Accounts of the Reeves and Bailiffs of the Dean and Chapter 1273–1364
HCA R121–95	Accounts of the Collectors of Common Rent of the Dean and Chapter 1290–1538
HCA R378–578	Accounts of the Receivers of Mass Pence 1285–1541
HCA R583–6, 2369, 2371	Accounts of the Clavigers 1477–1523
HCA R630–7, R637a–d, 1160, 4328	Accounts of the Masters of the Bakehouse of the Canons of the Cathedral 1294–1497

Miscellaneous documents and deeds:
HCA 766, 832, 1028, 1412, 1438, 1457, 1475, 1762, 1814, 1848, 2085A, 2086, 2236–7, 2252–3, 2316, 2457, 2465, 2467, 2473, 2595, 2780–1, 2787–91, 2799, 2822, 2844, 2868, 2880, 2885, 2891–3, 2898, 2923, 2974, 2990, 2994, 3011, 3155, 3194–5

Hereford Record Office

AL/19/6	Register of Bishop Mascall
AL/19/7	Register of Bishop Trefnant
AL/19/8	Register of Bishop Lacy
AL/19/12	Register of Bishop Mayew
AL/19/14	Register of Bishop Skip
AL/19/15	Register of Bishop Scory

The National Archives, Kew

PROB 11	Prerogative Court of Canterbury, registers of wills

Abbreviations

abp.	archbishop	ed.	edited by
adm.	admission, admit, admitted	edn.	edition
archdcn.	archdeacon	el.	elect, elected, election
archdcnry.	archdeaconry	enthr.	enthrone, enthroned, enthronement
BA	bachelor of arts		
BCL	bachelor of civil law	exch.	exchange, exchanged
BCnL	bachelor of canon law	excomm.	excommunicated, excommunication
Biog. ref.	Biographical reference/ references	expect.	expectative, provision to a canonry with expectation of a prebend
Bod. Lib.	Bodleian Library Oxford		
BM	bachelor of medicine		
BMus	bachelor of music	fo.	folio
bp.	bishop	gr.	grant, granted
bpc.	bishopric	instal.	installation, installed
BTh	bachelor of theology	instit.	admitted and instituted; institution
c.	*circa*		
can.	canon	judgt.	judgement
Cant.	Canterbury Cath. Library	k.	king
card.	cardinal	Lamb.	Lambeth Palace Library
cath.	cathedral	lic.	licence
ch.	church	LicCL	licenciate in civil law
chanc.	chancellor	lic. el.	licence to elect
chap.	chapel	LicTh	licenciate in theology
chapt.	chapter	M.	*magister*/master
coll.	collate, collated	m	mark, marks
colleg.	collegiate	MA	master of arts
comm.	commission	MD	doctor of medicine
conf.	confirmation, confirmed	m.i.	memorial/monumental inscription
cons.	consecration, consecrated		
ct.	court	mand.	mandate
d.	death, died	mand. adm.	mandate to admit
d. and c.	dean and chapter	mand. inq.	mandate for inquiry
DCL	doctor of civil law	MS.	manuscript
DCnL	doctor of canon law	n.d.	no date
dcn.	deacon	O.Can.S.A.	order of Augustinian canons
depriv.	deprive, deprived		
dig.	dignity	O.Carm.	order of Carmelites
dioc.	diocese	occ.	occurrence, occur, occurs
DMus	doctor of music	OFM	order of Friars Minor
DTh	doctor of theology	OP	order of Preachers

OSB	order of St Benedict	reservn.	reservation
prec.	precentor	RO	record office
preb.	prebend, prebendary	RS	Rolls Series
pres.	present, presentation,	SchTh	scholar of theology
	presented	s.d.	same day
prof. of obed.	profession of obedience	spirit.	spiritualities
prohibn.	prohibition	temps.	temporalities
prov.	provision, provided	treas.	treasurer
ratif.	ratified	TNA	The National Archives
reg.	register	trans.	translated, translation
res.	resign, resignation,	vac.	vacancy, vacant, vacated
	resigned	vic.	vicarage

Introduction

THE CHAPTER OF HEREFORD CATHEDRAL 1300–1541

The constitution and organization of the medieval chapter reached its final form in the mid thirteenth century, when the number of prebends was fixed and the statutes and liturgy were codified. The chapter consisted of four dignitaries, dean, precentor, treasurer and chancellor, two archdeacons, of Hereford and Shropshire, and twenty-eight canons. None of the canonries was attached to a dignity, and one, the prebendary of Episcopi, also acted as penitentiary. This was in almost all respects the standard pattern of English secular cathedrals. The differences were small: the treasurer had precedence over the chancellor, probably a reflection of late creation of the chancellorship at Hereford, and the subdean, as at Lichfield and St Paul's, was not a member of the chapter. With twenty-eight prebends Hereford was one of the smallest chapters: only Exeter had fewer, twenty-four; the four medium sized, Chichester, St Paul's, Lichfield and York, had thirty or more; and the largest, Lincoln, Salisbury and Wells, over fifty. The number at Hereford was fixed by papal decree in 1246 and closely reflects the number established in the late eleventh century by Bishop Robert the Lotharingian (1079–95), though their endowments were not finally fixed until the end of thirteenth century.[1] There were no subsequent constitutional changes to the chapter until after the Reformation; an attempt to attach the prebend of Bullinghope to the deanery between 1383 and 1397 was unsuccessful. The upheavals of the Henrician and Edwardian Reformations had remarkably little effect on this aspect of the cathedral and it was not until 1583 that there was constitutional change, when new statutes stipulated that there should be six residentiary canons.

In common with Chichester, Salisbury, Wells and York, Hereford had some prebends held by religious houses. This practice, which originated in the late twelfth and early thirteenth century, was a means of funding, and thereby increasing, the number of minor clergy who carried out much of the daily liturgy. The abbots of these houses became canons and provided vicars in their absence.[2] At Hereford two Norman abbeys, Cormeilles in 1195 and Lire in 1216 × 1219, made such arrangements. Their abbots became canons with a stall in the choir and a place in chapter like other canons, but they did not receive either small or greater

---

[1] The origins of Hereford's prebends are discussed in *Fasti Hereford 1066–1300* and J. Barrow, 'A Lotharingian at Hereford: Bishop Robert's reorganisation of the church of Hereford 1079–95', in *Medieval Art, Architecture and Archaeology in Hereford*, ed. D. Whitehead (British Archaeological Association Conference Transactions, xv, 1995) pp. 29–47.

[2] J. Barrow, 'The origins of vicars choral to *c*.1300', in *Cantate Domino: Vicars Choral at English Cathedrals*, ed. R. Hall and D. Stocker (Oxford, 2005) p. 15.

commons.[3] When present in the choir they were entitled to daily commons, a right which devolved to the two vicars each appointed, but compared with most monastic canonries at other English cathedrals their prebends were less clearly defined, simply consisting of the churches they held in the diocese.[4] It is for this reason that they are not separately listed in the *Fasti*. They were in effect honorary canons and had a purely nominal relationship with the cathedral, the most important element of which was the provision of four vicars choral. When the endowments of alien monastic houses were seized by the crown the patronage of Cormeilles passed to Fotheringhay College in 1411 and that of Lire to Sheen in 1414.[5] The transfer had very little impact at Hereford and vicars continued to be appointed.[6]

The medieval statutes date from their codification by Bishop Aigueblanche between 1246 and 1264, probably soon after 1246 following a series of papal confirmations of cathedral customs in 1245–6.[7] They are divided into two parts, the customs of the church and those of the choir. The former set out the installation of canons, their residence and emoluments, and the latter the duties and responsibilities of the dignitaries, vicars choral and other minor clergy. Aigueblanche's statutes formed the basis of cathedral life for the rest of the middle ages and were, as the first surviving chapter act book shows, still operating in the early sixteenth century.[8] This may partly explain why there was no further major statute making before the Reformation, whereas most other cathedrals continued to legislate.[9] There were, however, minor revisions and additions: in 1356 the level of learning required of the penitentiary was raised and in 1388 Dean Harold ruled that all canons had to give the cathedral a cope or 40s.[10] Bishop Aigueblanche's codification of the liturgy in the Hereford Breviary, which dates from 1262 × 8, was almost contemporary with his statute making and part of the same process of regulating cathedral life.

The chapter had an unusually high degree of independence from the bishop which it retained throughout the middle ages. The statutes sought to create an autonomous body and to avoid outside intervention in its affairs by urging canons to settle their disputes without appeal to a higher authority. This was not always possible; Bishop Mayew twice sought to mediate, in 1511 and 1513.[11] The independence of the chapter was most striking in its exemption from episcopal visitation which it maintained until the seventeenth century. This probably originated in grants made by Pope Innocent IV (1243–54). In October 1245 and April 1246 he confirmed the chapter's privileges but neither confirmation refers specifically to visitation rights.[12] However, episcopal visitation was one of the eighteen issues raised in a serious dispute between Bishop Aigueblanche and the chapter that was submitted

---

[3] *LS* II 59–60.

[4] Lists of the abbots of the two houses can be found in *Gallia Christiana* XI 644–51, 846–50.

[5] *CPR 1408–13* p. 358; *VCH Surrey* II 89.

[6] *Ch. & Rec.* pp. 270–1.

[7] These are printed in *LS* II 44–89 and summarized and discussed in J. Barrow, 'The constitution of Hereford cathedral in the thirteenth century', in G. Aylmer and J. Tiller, *Hereford Cathedral: a History* (2000) pp. 633–6.

[8] HCA 7031/1 fos. 3–11.

[9] D. N. Lepine, *A Brotherhood of Canons Serving God* (Woodbridge, 1995) pp. 88–90.

[10] *Ch. & Rec.* pp. 228–9; *LS* II 86–7. Bishop Mayew confirmed this in 1524 (HCA 3186).

[11] *Reg. Mayew* pp. 112–13, 181–5.

[12] *Reg. Innocent IV* no. 1591; *Ch. & Rec.* pp. 78–80.

for papal arbitration in 1252. One of the bishop's complaints was that the chapter had not allowed him to exercise his right as the diocesan to visit the cathedral. The papal arbitrators broadly found in favour of the chapter but did not rule explicitly on most issues, including visitation rights, instead upholding the position before the dispute and requiring the bishop not to press his claims.[13] This award seems to have been the basis of the chapter's subsequent claim of exemption. When successfully resisting Bishop Spofford's attempt to carry out a visitation in 1427 the chapter cited the 'register of St Richard, former bishop of Hereford' as evidence of their privilege.[14] This was probably the 1252 award and the reference to St Richard was a corruption of the name of the principal papal arbitrator 'Ricardum, sancti Angeli diaconum cardinalum', Riccardo Annibaldi, cardinal deacon of St Angelo in Pescheria (d. 1276).[15] Although Bishop Orleton secured a papal bull in 1320 which gave him authority to visit the cathedral he did not implement it.[16] In 1522 Bishop Booth was no more successful than Bishop Spofford had been in 1427 in pressing episcopal claims.[17] Only Bishop Beauchamp seems to have succeeded in 1450 but no account has survived and no precedent was set.[18] The chapter remained exempt from visitation by the diocesan until new statutes were issued in 1636. Even so a visitation was not carried out until 1677.[19] No other chapter had such an exemption. The chapter had less success in resisting the claim of the archbishop of Canterbury to visit the cathedral in his capacity as metropolitan. Both Archbishop Pecham in 1282 and Cardinal Pole in 1556 carried out visitations, the former despite an appeal by the chapter to the pope.[20] Archbishop Courtenay's attempt in 1396 might have succeeded despite a challenge by Bishop Trefnant had it not been cut short by his death, but the chapter was able to frustrate Archbishop Arundel in 1404.[21]

The major constitutional developments of the later medieval period concerned the minor clergy rather than the canons, the most significant of which was the incorporation of the vicars choral. Hereford had fewer minor clergy than most other cathedrals and they were organized differently. The four ranks generally found in England, vicars choral, chantry priests, secondaries and choristers, were less distinct and there were no secondaries, but Hereford, in common with St Paul's, had minor canons. As Julia Barrow has shown, the evolution of minor clergy at cathedrals was a more complex and varied process than previously thought.[22] At Hereford four types of vicar can be identified, deputies of the dignitaries, those provided by religious houses, Bishop Maidstone's Diddlebury foundation and those with chantry responsibilities as well as choir duties. The Hereford vicars choral were the responsibility of the chapter and not deputies appointed by canons, many

---

[13] *Ch. & Rec.* pp. 95–101.

[14] *Reg. Spofford* p. 102.

[15] *Ch. & Rec.* p. 99.

[16] *CPL* II 196.

[17] *Reg. Booth* pp. 130–2.

[18] *Reg. Beauchamp* p. 11.

[19] S. Lehmberg with G. Aylmer, 'Reformation to Restoration, 1535–1660', in Aylmer and Tiller, *Hereford Cathedral* pp. 94–9.

[20] *Ibid.*; *Reg. Pecham* II 176–7, 181, 186, 188–9; HCA 1550.

[21] *Reg. Trefnant* pp. 120–5; *Ch. & Rec.* pp. 256–8.

[22] Barrow, 'Origins of vicars choral' pp. 13–15.

of whose prebends were too small to support one. By 1300 there were about twenty-four.[23] In 1327–30 there was a substantial increase of ten, eight priests, a deacon and a subdeacon, as a result of the gift of the advowson of Lugwardine, Herefs., by Joanne de Bohun and Thomas Chaundos, archdeacon of Hereford.[24] This new total of thirty-four was probably sustained until the Black Death but numbers had fallen to twenty-seven in 1395, twenty-one in 1407 and twenty in 1535, though there were twenty-five in 1411.[25] Financial insecurity was a major reason for this decline and remained a preoccupation for the rest of the medieval period. In 1384 Bishop Gilbert attempted to appropriate the church of Westbury, Glos., valued at £53 6s 8d in 1291, to the vicars, but their right to hold property was uncertain. The resolution of this problem led to the incorporation of the vicars into a college in 1395 when the church was finally appropriated.[26] Nearly a century later, in 1472–5, an impressive new college was built for them. However, their financial difficulties persisted and in 1487 a papal dispensation was granted allowing vicars to hold other benefices without residing in them because of their poverty.[27] Many held chantries in the cathedral; in 1535 fourteen of the twenty-one chantries were held by vicars.[28] As a result of their origins and subsequent poverty the distinction between vicars and chantry priests was more blurred during the later middle ages than at other cathedrals.

There was little change for the rest of the minor clergy. Hereford's chantry priests were not provided with separate accommodation or incorporated, unlike those at Exeter, Lichfield, Lincoln, St Paul's, Wells and York. In the early sixteenth century the organization of the choristers became more centralized and they acquired their own accommodation but there were still only five as late as 1512–13.[29] The minor or petty canons at Hereford seem to have been a fifteenth-century development. Six are listed in 1535 in the *Valor Ecclesiasticus*, all of whom were vicars, and in 1536 Bishop Fox referred to four minor canons and two others called 'Dudleburys'.[30] They were the six most senior vicars, distinguished by a higher salary and, by at least 1525, their own robes.[31] Their origins may date back to the original foundation of the vicars in the early thirteenth century. The mid thirteenth-century statutes single out four priest vicars and in 1294–5 the four vicars appointed by the abbeys of Cormeilles and Lire are called the four senior vicars, 'quatuor maiorum vicarorum'.[32] From 1463–4, but not in 1425–6, they are regularly called the canons of Cormeilles and Lire but it is not clear when the two 'Dudleburys' were given this status or why it evolved.[33]

[23] *Fasti Hereford 1066–1300* pp. xxviii–xxx.

[24] *Ch. & Rec.* pp. 208–9, 210–15; *Reg. T. Charlton* pp. 16–17, 34–40.

[25] *Ch. & Rec.* p. 253; TNA, E 179/30/21; *Valor* III 12; *Reg. Mascall* p. 79.

[26] *Reg. Gilbert* pp. 46–7; *Ch. & Rec.* pp. 253–5.

[27] *Reg. Mayew* pp. 15–18.

[28] *Valor* III 13–15.

[29] N. I. Orme, 'The cathedral school before the Reformation', in Aylmer and Tiller, *Hereford Cathedral* pp. 567–73; HCA R585 fo. 15r.

[30] *Reg. Booth* p. 365.

[31] *Valor* III 12; HCA 7031/1 fo. 36v.

[32] *LS* II 75; HCA R631.

[33] HCA R637, 637a, 637b, 4328.

In theory the bishop appointed all members of the chapter except the dean, who was elected; at Hereford he also allocated canons' houses in the close. In practice there were many demands on episcopal patronage which were hard to resist: from the crown, lay magnates, fellow bishops and, in the fourteenth century, the papacy, as well as ambitious clerics themselves. Access to all four routes lay through the networks of patronage and kinship at the heart of medieval society. Bishop Swinfield's register is unusually revealing of the pressures faced by bishops. As well as repeated royal demands and papal provisions, he received requests from aspiring clerics and his episcopal colleagues.[34] Royal appointments were based on the exercise of 'regalian right' by which the king discharged the bishop's patronage during a vacancy.[35] In the fourteenth century this was extended beyond vacancies. At Hereford the scale of interventions outside vacancies was small, an average of one every three years, nearly two-thirds of which were ineffective.[36] However, episcopal vacancies were more fully and successfully exploited; thirty-six grants were made in the period 1317–1538, nearly two-thirds of which were effective. They were concentrated in the fourteenth century when between four and six were made during most vacancies, and as many as ten in 1360–1 when the vacancy was prolonged by a disputed election.[37] Direct intervention, even during vacancies, was rare in the fifteenth century but royal pressure on appointments did not cease, it became less visible. Though few letters of recommendation have survived, the presence of so many royal clerks among the chapter in the fifteenth century suggests that bishops found it hard to resist the crown's demands. Royal influence also extended to papal provisions, many of which were made at the king's request.

Papal intervention was a major limitation of episcopal patronage in the fourteenth century, though one which bishops, like the king, came to use to their advantage to promote their own clerks. It was based on the pope's claim of *plenitudio potestatis* which included the right to appoint to all benefices in Christendom. This took two principal forms when applied to cathedrals: provision to a named, usually vacant, prebend or dignity; and provision to a canonry with an expectation of an unnamed prebend or dignity.[38] Hereford's remoteness and relative poverty did not exempt it from papal intervention though it received fewer provisions than other chapters of comparable size and status.[39] There were 122 provisions and expectations to Hereford prebends and dignities in the period 1300–1541, the first in 1306 and the last in 1398. They were concentrated in the episcopates of Thomas Charlton (1327–44), John Trillek (1344–60) and especially the relatively short ones of Lewis Charlton (1361–9) and William Courtenay (1370–5). They were not predominantly made to wealthier dignities or prebends, as most were expectations to unnamed prebends. Even so, just over half, fifty-five per cent, were successful. Provisions were made on a large enough scale at Hereford in the mid fourteenth century to make significant inroads into episcopal patronage.

[34] *Reg. Swinfield* pp. 1–2, 7, 135, 150–3, 286, 443–5, 482–3, 513.

[35] Lepine, *Brotherhood of Canons* pp. 24–8.

[36] There were thirty-two between 1308 and 1396 of which twenty were ineffective.

[37] No grants were made in the 1327 and 1375 vacancies.

[38] J. R. Wright, *The Church and the English Crown 1305–34* (Toronto, 1980) pp. 5–26.

[39] *Ibid.* p. 282.

Evidence of direct pressure from lay magnates at Hereford is rare, but undated letters of recommendation and thanks for the appointment of William Ashton (*fl.* 1376) to the prebend of Hunderton from the countess of March suggest that it was standard practice.[40] Exchange was the only route to a canonry that did not need the support of a patron, though in theory the bishop's approval was necessary to effect one.[41] Once in possession of a benefice a cleric could exchange it for a canonry. This tended to be done either by ambitious clerics for immediate career advantage, sometimes for financial gain, or by those anxious to settle at the cathedral. There were ninety-seven exchanges in the period 1300–1541, twenty-three of which were of dignities. They were most frequent from the 1340s to the 1440s when there were between four and eight per decade, with a notable peak between 1360 and 1390. Relatively few, eighteen, involved other prebends or dignities in the cathedral. Though it was common for canons to move from one prebend to another, usually to a richer one, at Hereford this was generally effected by resignation and episcopal collation rather than by direct exchange between canons.

Despite having some of the poorest prebends in England, Hereford canonries were sought after. Two canons went so far as to be accused of resorting to simony to gain one: Roger Braynton, albeit posthumously in 1356, and Hugh Grene in 1508–11.[42] All Hereford's prebends, whatever their value, conferred status and attracted some of the most successful clerics of their day. Competition for prebends resulted in disputes and in the most serious cases litigation. This was greatest in the fourteenth century when it was exacerbated by the alternative routes available, especially royal grants and papal provisions. In many cases rivals had as competing patrons either the king or the pope. Disputes were generally confined to dignities and richer prebends such as Bullinghope and Moreton Magna, but not exclusively. Hunderton, Putson Minor, Warham and Withington Parva, all worth less than £10, were the subject of disputes. The most notorious was John Middleton's unsuccessful attempt to gain the deanery *c.*1380–2. Middleton was accused of arranging an exchange when the incumbent, William Birmingham, was senile and of fraudulently obtaining a papal provision. Some disputes were prolonged: the chancellorship remained vacant for twelve years between 1375 and 1387 partly because of competing royal and papal claims, and the prebend of Hunderton, valued at only £5 8s in 1291, was the subject of unresolved competing claims for more than twenty-five years from 1349 to 1376. There were few disputes in the fifteenth century because the competing methods of appointment were curtailed, the crown rarely intervened openly and from the 1390s papal provisions were blocked. Compared with wealthier cathedrals with richer prebends Hereford had fewer and less acrimonious disputes.

Hereford was one of the poorest secular cathedrals. The 1291 *Taxatio* values the common fund at about £365 and the prebends at about £228 but is less precise about the dignities.[43] These, excluding the archdeaconries, are valued in 1294

---

[40] HCA 2968, 3189.

[41] Lepine, *Brotherhood of Canons* pp. 36–8.

[42] *Reg. Trillek* pp. 244–5; *Reg. Mayew* pp. 34–47, 103–4.

[43] R. N. Swanson and D. N. Lepine, 'The later middle ages 1268–1535', in Aylmer and Tiller, *Hereford Cathedral* p. 51; *Taxatio* pp. 157–60, 168–70.

at £80.[44] The *Valor Ecclesiasticus* gives different but broadly similar figures. The common fund is valued at £423 17s 2¼d net, the prebends at £234 5s, the dignities at £89 16s 10½d and the archdeaconries at £74 8s 8d.[45] The *Valor* enables comparisons with other secular cathedrals to be made. In 1535 Hereford was the second poorest of the nine in its total income, the value of its common fund and prebends, and the incomes of its vicars and chantry priests, and the poorest in the value of its dignities and archdeaconries.[46] Although its economic history has yet to be written, surviving accounts show that the cathedral's revenues fell after the Black Death and arrears accumulated.[47] There were few new endowments after 1300 to compensate for this, a steady accumulation of small sums to fund chantries and obits but only four substantial grants. In 1320 Bishop Orleton granted the church of Shinfield, Berks., an episcopal possession since 1269, to the fabric fund.[48] The vicars received two gifts, Lugwardine in 1327–30 and Westbury in 1395, and in 1525 St Ethelbert's Hospital, Hereford, was united with the treasurership on account of the latter's poverty.[49] These four endowments were valued at £106 5s 2d in 1535.[50] In addition the cathedral received a considerable income from pilgrims to the shrine of St Thomas Cantilupe in the early fourteenth century but this was a much smaller and less reliable source of revenue for the rest of the middle ages.[51]

Hereford's prebends were notoriously meagre.[52] It had the three poorest in England, Episcopi, which had no endowment, and Pratum Majus and Pratum Minus, valued at 2d and 6d respectively in 1291. In the 1291 valuation seventeen of the twenty-eight prebends (sixty per cent) were worth less than £10. Only four were worth £15–20 in 1291 and none over £20. By 1535 the *Valor Ecclesiasticus* shows that, overall, little had changed, though the two valuations are not strictly comparable as the *Valor* includes small commons, worth 37s 8½d that year, in its valuation of the prebends. There were still fifteen prebends worth less than £10. But the *Valor* also reveals that Hereford was not unique in this respect. At Chichester, Lichfield and St Paul's between a third and a half of the prebends were worth less than £10 and at Wells over half were.[53] The reason for the relative poverty of Hereford's prebends lies in their origins. Most were modestly endowed from estates rather than churches, which were generally of greater value, and Hereford was less able than other cathedrals to attract gifts of prebendal endowments from outsiders.[54] Hereford was unusual in the location of its prebends, the majority of which were close to the city. Eight were in the city or its immediate environs,[55] and another

---

[44] *Reg. Swinfield* p. 305.
[45] *Valor* III 4–10.
[46] S. E. Lehmberg, *The Reformation of the Cathedrals* (Princeton, 1988) pp. 26–8.
[47] Swanson and Lepine, 'The later middle ages' pp. 52–4.
[48] *Ch. & Rec.* pp. 123, 184–6; *Reg. Orleton* pp. 149–50, 158–61.
[49] See nn. 24 and 26 above; *Reg. Booth* pp. 171–2.
[50] Shinfield was valued at £20, Lugwardine at £32 3s 4d, Westbury at £44 and St Ethelbert's Hospital at £10 1s 10d (*Valor* III 5, 8).
[51] Swanson and Lepine, 'The later middle ages' pp. 72–6.
[52] Individual valuations are given at the beginning of each list below.
[53] *Valor* I 134–7, 300–2, 363–5, III 130–2.
[54] *Fasti Hereford 1066–1300* p. xxvi; Barrow, 'A Lotharingian in Hereford' pp. 37–41.
[55] Bartonsham, Bullinghope, Eign, Hinton, Hunderton, Huntingdon, Putson Minor and Warham.

nine were within five miles of the cathedral.[56] Four were slightly more distant, seven miles from Hereford,[57] and only three were a substantial distance: Colwall, on the Malvern Hills, Inkberrow, east of Worcester, and Moreton and Whaddon, south of Gloucester. Only St Paul's had a similar concentration of prebends close to the cathedral.

The low value of many Hereford prebends was partly compensated for by the commons to which canons were entitled. There were three types, small, greater and daily. All canons, whether resident or not, received small commons consisting of distributions of grain and 20s a year. Greater commons were paid in grain twice a year to residentiaries who were also entitled to a share of any surplus income from chapter estates. Daily commons were paid in two forms to those present at the liturgy: bread and grain in lieu of ale for those attending matins, and mass pence for those attending mass, initially 4d but 1¼d by the 1450s. The labyrinthine complexities of the accounting system used by the chapter make it difficult to quantify canons' income with any precision. It is also difficult to give a cash value of the bread and grain received by residentiaries. Even so, some estimates can be hazarded: in the 1290s residentiaries received between £3 and £6 in mass pence but this had fallen to 20–30s in the 1450s; in the first half of the fourteenth century the annual surplus distributed to each residentiary by the collectors of the common rents ranged from 12s to 30s; and in 1535 small commons was valued at 37s 8½d.[58]

The Hereford chapter, like those of the other eight secular cathedrals, was dominated by members of the higher clergy, the elite of the late medieval church. They were able, educated and established clerics, with successful careers in the service of the church or crown. Geographically Hereford drew many of its canons from within the diocese: in the period 1258–1541 nearly a third of those with known geographical origins (some two-thirds of canons).[59] The strength of the cathedral's influence is clearer still from a regional analysis; forty-two per cent came from the Severn and Wye valleys, the counties of Herefordshire, Worcestershire, Gloucestershire, Shropshire and Monmouthshire. This commitment to the cathedral was strongest among the residentiaries, nearly two-thirds of whom were from the diocese and three-quarters from the Severn and Wye valleys. Foreign canons were rare after 1300, and confined to a handful of French and Italians. Welshmen, though, were more numerous, outnumbering those from the diocese of York. These aspiring Welsh clerics looked to Hereford and England for advancement. New men were brought into the chapter when the bishop originated from outside the diocese: Bishop Swinfield (1283–1317) brought an influx from his native Kent, and Bishop Spofford (1422–48) one from Yorkshire.

Although we know relatively little about their social origins, it is clear that the chapter was mainly drawn from the upper, landowning, levels of medieval society.

---

[56] Church Withington, Ewithington, Hampton, Moreton Magna and Parva, Nonnington, Pratum Majus, Pratum Minus and Withington Parva.

[57] Gorwell, Pion Parva, Preston and Wellington.

[58] HCA R 381, 491–8; HCA R129–36; *Valor* III 9.

[59] This and the next nine paragraphs are a revised summary of Swanson and Lepine, 'The later middle ages' pp. 54–67, which should be consulted for further detail and references.

A handful were born into baronial families, especially ones from the diocese; members of the Charlton, Mortimer and Talbot families were a significant presence in the fourteenth-century chapter. Those from the lesser aristocracy, from the ranks of knight, esquire and gentleman, were a larger and more influential group, especially the sons of local families, few of whom were unrepresented in the course of the later middle ages: among them the Barres, Baskervilles, Burleys, Caples, Chaundoses, Delaberes, Hacluits, Pembridges, Vaughans, Whitneys and Walwayns. Their membership strengthened the local roots of the cathedral and reinforced its standing in the diocese. Less prominent landowners, what might be described as the parish gentry of the Severn and Wye valleys, were also plentiful. Those from an urban background also came largely from its upper levels, the merchants and master craftsmen who made up the ruling oligarchy, but until the early sixteenth century relatively few were from leading Hereford families. None of the chapter is known to have come from a non-landowning or poor urban background.

Graduates dominated the chapter; two-thirds had a university education. After 1450 it was increasingly rare for non-graduates to be appointed. More than half the graduates gained a higher degree, with nearly thirty per cent having doctorates. Their choice of study was strongly practical, with law dominating: forty-five per cent of graduates studied either civil or canon law. For the ambitious cleric there were many opportunities in royal and diocesan administration for the legal graduate. Theologians were relatively few and far between and before the sixteenth century scarce among the residentiaries. The overwhelming majority of graduates studied at Oxford, reflecting its strong links with the west of England from where it recruited many of its students; only a handful attended Cambridge or foreign universities.

By the time they received their prebends most Hereford canons, as many as two-thirds, were experienced royal or ecclesiastical administrators. Service to the king occupied over a quarter of the chapter, many of them non-residents though some retired to the cathedral close at the end of their careers. An even greater proportion, over a third, were engaged in ecclesiastical service. Diocesan administrators were usually among the first to be rewarded with canonries by grateful bishops; virtually all senior office-holders gained prebends. At Hereford twenty per cent were in the bishop's service and as many as three-quarters of these entered residence, thereby demonstrating a strong commitment both to the diocese and the cathedral. The rest were employed by other diocesans, the Canterbury and York administrations, or the pope. Magnate service was a third but less widespread form of employment. Some resident canons had particularly close links with leading families in the diocese, holding positions of trust as executors or feoffees.

The resident canons formed the core of the cathedral, leading the worship, supervising the administration and dispensing hospitality. During the thirteenth century all chapters made a clear distinction between residents and non-residents, accepting the fact that a significant proportion of the chapter would be absent on royal or ecclesiastical business. Residence and participation in the liturgy were encouraged by setting aside part of the chapter's resources, the common fund, to make payments to residentiaries. At Hereford, to qualify for full residence a canon had to be present for thirty-six weeks a year and to attend matins each day. The sixteen weeks' absence allowed could not be taken consecutively. These were among the most rigorous requirements at any cathedral but in return residentiaries received the relatively generous emoluments outlined above.

Residence flourished from the 1270s to the 1330s when between a third and a half of the chapter, ten to fourteen canons, were resident.[60] In peak years there were sixteen or seventeen canons present in the cathedral close and occasionally, in the 1290s, as many as twenty. This was a period of economic prosperity and vigorous activity in the cathedral, when it was an important pilgrim shrine and also a time of major rebuilding. Some decline occurred in the 1340s, before the Black Death, when numbers fell to ten or eleven. This level was sustained until the beginning of the fifteenth century. A further decline set in during the mid 1410s after which it was unusual for there to be more than seven resident, a quarter of the chapter. From the 1420s to the 1530s there were usually between four and eight canons in residence. The 1420s to the early 1450s were difficult years, with only four or five resident, but for the next forty years, until the early 1490s, there were often seven present. There was another lean period from the mid 1490s for a decade, when there might be only three residentiaries, followed by some recovery after 1505 to between six and eight. Apart from a temporary falling off in the later 1520s this level was sustained until 1540. Residence was by no means moribund at Hereford on the eve of the Reformation. Compared with other cathedrals residence levels at Hereford were healthy but not outstanding. Overall, almost a third of the chapter entered residence, though for much of the fifteenth and early sixteenth centuries the average was a quarter. Hereford never reached the sustained high levels found at Exeter and Wells but matched the moderate levels found at Lincoln, Salisbury and Lichfield and avoided the persistently low ones of St Paul's and York.

The resident chapter at Hereford was never as distinguished as the community of scholars that flourished at Salisbury in the first half of the fifteenth century. Its membership was mainly drawn from able local men engaged in diocesan administration. Though remote, it was not entirely a provincial backwater, and some outstanding figures came to Hereford, among them the chronicler Adam Murimuth and the scholar Thomas Chaundler. The resident community in the half century after 1450 shows the chapter at its best, a body of conscientious and learned ecclesiastics such as Richard Rudhale (d. 1476), a loyal episcopal servant many of whose carefully annotated books are still in the library. Like many residentiaries he was buried in the cathedral, established an obit in it and was a generous benefactor.[61] In these ways residentiaries acknowledged the importance of the cathedral in their lives as the focus of their devotion and the source of their income and status.

It has generally been assumed that non-resident canons had little contact with their cathedrals and their critics have characterized them as absentee drones taking the income of their prebends but contributing little in return. The detail of the Hereford accounts enables us to see a more complete picture. Nearly half, forty-two per cent, of non-residents visited the cathedral, most of them taking the

---

[60] The methods used for calculating residence levels and the particular problems encountered at Hereford are set out in Lepine, *Brotherhood of Canons* pp. 199–200.

[61] D. N. Lepine, 'A long way from university: cathedral canons and learning at Hereford in the fifteenth century', in *The Church and Learning in Late Medieval Society*, ed. C. Barron and J. Stratford (Donnington, 2002) pp. 178–95.

trouble to be installed personally and some practising what amounted to partial residence, regularly spending up to three months a year at Hereford. Though many non-residents had little to do with the cathedral, the chapter found them useful as it was able to seek advice from senior and influential officials. Hereford's location on the Welsh marches gave the chapter a political role in times of disturbance. Several canons, mainly non-residentiaries, were actively involved in the administration of the marcher lordship as commissioners of the peace for Herefordshire and at a more senior level as members of the council of the marches and the household of Prince Arthur at Ludlow.[62] Richard Kingston, archdeacon of Hereford and keeper of the wardrobe, co-ordinated Henry IV's response to Owain Glyn Dwr's revolt in 1402–3 from the city.[63]

The Hereford chapter, like the other eight, was a privileged corporation. The chapter collectively, and to a lesser extent individual prebendaries, had secular and ecclesiastical jurisdiction over their estates and churches, including the city of Hereford where there was a complex jurisdictional pattern.[64] The dean's peculiar jurisdiction covered the rural deanery of Hereford, known as the cathedral deanery, consisting of the six city parishes and a further thirty-one outside it. In addition, the cathedral had the unusual and lucrative privilege of having sole burial rights in the city; only Exeter and Lichfield had similar rights. The cathedral cemetery was the principal burial ground in Hereford and the chapter went to great lengths and expense to preserve its rights in an eighteen year dispute with the vicar of St Peter's, Hereford, but with only partial success.[65] Hereford was also unusual – one of only four cathedrals – in having a parish altar, the altar of St John the Baptist, located in the nave.[66] The cathedral close was the last to be formally enclosed, receiving a licence to 'close the cemetery with strong gates' in November 1389 in response to the 'theft, secret burials, animal grazing which dug up corpses, and frequent immorality'.[67] There is some uncertainty over the extent to which the close was enclosed both before and after 1389. There were already gates when the licence was granted; a document dated December 1389 refers to a western gate and the great gate, and in 1434 Bishop Spofford, complaining about the desecration of the close, ordered the gates to be properly closed.[68]

Sources
Both the diocese of Hereford and its cathedral have rich medieval archives which together with the royal and papal records enable a substantially complete *Fasti* to be compiled. However, significant gaps of a decade or more remain for most

---

[62] Richard Martin, Thomas Chaundler, John Arundel and John Hervy (*CPR 1467–77* p. 616; *CPR 1476–85* p. 561; *CPR 1485–94* p. 488; *CPR 1494–1509* p. 642). Richard Martin was a member of the former and John Argentine the latter (*BRUO* II 1236–7; *BRUC* pp. 15–16).

[63] *CPR 1401–5* pp. 91, 135, 293, 439; *Ch. & Rec.* pp. 255–6.

[64] Swanson and Lepine, 'The later middle ages' pp. 78–9.

[65] W. J. Dohar, *The Black Death and Pastoral Leadership: the Diocese of Hereford in the Fourteenth Century* (Philadelphia, 1995) pp. 82–6.

[66] D. N. Lepine, 'And alle oure paresshens: secular cathedrals and parish churches in late medieval England', in *The Parish in Late Medieval England*, ed. C. Burgess and E. Duffy (Donnington, 2006) pp. 31–2.

[67] *CPR 1388–92* p. 160.

[68] HCA 2944; *Reg. Spofford* pp. 180–2.

prebends. The bishops' registers survive in an almost complete sequence from 1275, the only break being from 1492 to 1504, during the episcopates of Audley and Castello, and all were printed in the early twentieth century. However, these editions do not use modern editorial conventions and are poorly indexed. Royal and papal records provide essential additional material particularly for the fourteenth century when both the crown and papacy intervened directly in the appointment of canons. The first edition of the Hereford *Fasti* relied on the Bliss calendars of papal letters and petitions. Since its publication significantly more of the papal archives has become available. The full printed editions of the original papal registers, an ongoing project by the Bibliothèque des Ecoles Françaises d'Athènes et de Rome, which were not used in the first edition, and Lunt's and Graves's edition of the accounts of the papal collectors in England have greatly increased our knowledge of the scale of papal provisions to English cathedrals. In addition there has been a steady increase in other relevant printed sources since 1962, not least more than twenty-five episcopal registers.

For all the richness of the cathedral's medieval archive, problems arise when using it to understand the chapter's history in this period. The first surviving chapter act book dates from 1512 leaving no evidence for most of the later middle ages. Although there are more than 400 surviving medieval account rolls, excluding manorial accounts, Hereford's accounting system has rightly been described as 'among the most complicated in use at any English secular cathedral'.[69] Six principal sets of accounts survive, often in long runs: for the reeves and bailiffs, the collectors of common rents, the receivers of mass pence, the receivers of heriots and oblations, the masters of the canons' bakehouse and the clavigers. The endowments, income and expenditure of each were accounted for separately and no central accounts were kept. While several of these list residentiaries, the most useful for compiling the *Fasti* are the accounts of the receivers of mass pence which record attendance at the daily mass by both resident and non-resident canons. None of the accounts contains full lists of canons; they were solely concerned with those entitled to a share of their income. The only documents containing complete lists are records of decanal elections. A further difficulty is created by the practice of referring to canons only by their surnames, sometimes an abbreviated version, without listing their prebends or dignities. This has resulted in a long list of canons with unidentified prebends. The wealth of Hereford deeds, charters and other documents – some 5,000 have survived – enables some gaps to be filled. A detailed calendar by B. G. Charles and H. D. Emmanuel can be found in the National Register of Archives, now at The National Archives, Kew and in Hereford Cathedral Library. A selection of these was published by W. Capes in 1908, but with few dating from after 1400.

---

[69] K. Edwards, *The English Secular Cathedrals in the Middle Ages* (Manchester, 1967) p. 242.

Hereford Diocese 1300–1541

BISHOPS

The temps. of the see were valued at £452 12s 5d in 1291 (*Taxatio* p. 168). The receiver of the bpc. rendered accounts for year ending 29 Sept. 1534 of £667 12s 1¾d, plus £170 6s 6½d profits of commissary and vicar-general and £11 18s 8d from registrar (total £849 17s 4½d) (*L&P* VII no. 1203). In 1535 the bpc. was valued at £768 10s 10¾d (*Valor* III 1–4).

M. Richard de Swinfield DTh 1282–1317

El. 1 Oct. 1282 (*Reg. Swinfield* p. 273). Abp's conf., and spirit. 31 Dec. (*Registrum Epistolarum J. Peckham* (RS 77) pp. 498–9; *Reg. Peckham* II 185). Temps. 8 Jan 1283 (*CPR 1281–92* p. 54). Lic. *alibi consecrari* 5 March (Cant., Reg. A fo. 84b/99b). Cons. 7 March; prof. of obed. to Canterbury s.d. (*ibid.* fo. 273b/233b). D. 15 March 1317 (*BRUO* III 1033; Lamb. MS. 20 fo. 172b). Biog. ref.: *BRUO* III 1833–4; P. Hoskin, 'Swinfield, Richard (d. 1317)', *ODNB* <http://www.oxforddnb.com/view/article/26843>.

M. Adam Orleton DCnL 1317–27

Lic. el. 7 Apr. 1317 (*CPR 1313–17* p. 633). Prov. 15 May in spite of mand. from k. 6 May to decline appointment (*CPL* II 150; *Feodera* II i 125). Cons. 22 May (*Registrum Sacrum Anglicanum*, ed. W. Stubbs (Oxford 1897) p. 71). Prof. of obed. 30 June (Cant., Reg. A fo. 273b/233b). Spirit. 2 July (*Reg. Orleton* p. 1). Temps. 24 July (*ibid.* p. 16; *CPR 1317–21* p. 3). Enthr. 2 Oct. (*Reg. Orleton* p. 33). Edward II confiscated the temps. March 1324 and kept them until Orleton trans. to Worcester 1327. Also held unidentified preb. Biog. ref.: *BRUO* II 1402–4; R. M. Haines, 'Orleton, Adam (*c.*1275–1345)', *ODNB* <http://www.oxforddnb.com/view/article/96>.

M. Thomas Charlton DCL 1327–44

Prov. 25 Sept. (*CPL* II 263). Cons. 18 Oct. (Murimuth, *Continuatio Chronicarum* (RS 93) p. 58. Prof. of obed. 30 Nov. (Cant., Reg. A fo. 274/234). Temps. 21 Dec. (*CPR 1327–30* p. 195). D. 11 Jan. 1344 (*BRUO* I 393). Also preb. of Church Withington. Biog. ref.: *BRUO* I 392–3; D. Lepine, 'Charlton, Thomas (*c.*1292–1344)', *ODNB* <http://www.oxforddnb.com/view/article/5168>.

M. John Trillek 1344–60

Lic. el. 27 Jan. 1344 (*CPR 1343–4* p. 189). El. 22 Feb. (*Reg. Trillek* p. 1). Royal assent 5 March (*CPR 1343–4* p. 216). Prov. 15 March (*CPL* III 95). Abp.'s conf. 27 March (*Reg. Trillek* p. 1). Temps. 29 March (*CPR 1343–4* p. 222). Cons 29 Aug.

(*Eubel* I 274). Enthr. 24 Oct. (*Reg. Trillek* p. 21). Prof. of obed. 9 Sept. 1348 (Cant., Reg. A fo. 274/234). Incapacitated by 1359 and d. 20 Nov. 1360 (*CPR 1358–61* pp. 326–7; *Reg. L. Charlton* p. 38). Also preb. of Putson Major and Wellington. Biog. ref.: *BRUO* III 1906; D. Lepine, 'Trillek, John (*c.*1308–60)', *ODNB* <http://www. oxforddnb.com/view/article/95146>.

M. John Barnet senior BCL 1360
M. Lewis Charlton LicTh 1361–9

Lic. el. 13 Dec. 1360 (*CPR 1358–61* p. 507). Disputed el., part of chapt. el. Barnet, the other part Charlton (Lamb., Reg. Islip fo. 231). Prov. to Charlton at k.'s request 10 Sept. 1361 (*ibid.*; *Original Papal Letters in England 1305–1415*, ed. P. N. R. Zutshi (Index Actorum Romanorum Pontificum, v, Vatican City, 1990) no. 272). Cons. 25 Oct. (*Reg. L. Charlton* p. 1). Prof. of obed. and spirit. 3 Nov. (Lamb., Reg. Islip fo. 181/183). Temps. 14 Nov. (*CPR 1361–4* p. 106). D. 23 May 1369 (*Reg. L. Charlton* p. 1). Charlton also preb. of Wellington. Biog. ref.: Barnet, *BRUO* I 112–13; W. M. Ormrod, 'Barnet, John (d. 1373)', *ODNB* <http://www.oxforddnb.com/view/article/1476>; Charlton, *BRUO* I 391–2; W. J. Dohar, 'Charlton, Lewis (d. 1369)', *ODNB* <http://www.oxforddnb.com/view/article/5166>.

Thomas Brantingham 1369
M. William Courtenay DCL 1369–75

Lic. el. 8 July 1369 (*CPR 1367–70* p. 282). Brantingham el. n.d. (*Reg. Brantingham* p. 745). Prov. to Courtenay 17 Aug. (*Reg. Courtenay* p. 2). Cons. 17 March 1370 (*Eubel* I 274). Temps. 19 March (*CPR 1367–70* p. 379). Enthr. 15 Sept. (*Reg. Courtenay* pp. 4–5). Prof. of obed. 13 Nov. 1372 (Lamb., Reg. Wittlesey fo. 58). Trans. to London 1375. Brantingham also preb. of Ewithington. Biog. ref.: Brantingham, R. G. Davies, 'Brantingham, Thomas (d. 1394)', *ODNB* <http://www.oxforddnb.com/view/article/3278>; Courtenay, *BRUO* I 502–4; R. N. Swanson, 'Courtenay, William (1341/2–96)', *ODNB* <http://www.oxforddnb.com/view/article/6457>.

M. John Gilbert OP, BTh 1375–89

Trans. from Bangor 12 Sept. 1375 (Lamb., Reg. Sudbury fo. 22b). Temps. 4 Dec. (*CPR 1374–7* p. 199). Spirit. 6 Dec. (Lamb., Reg. Sudbury fos. 22b, 23). Trans. to St Davids 1389. Biog. ref.: *BRUO* II 765–6.

M. John Trefnant DCL 1389–1404

Prov. 5 May 1389 (*Reg. Trefnant* p. 1). Cons. 20 June (*ibid.* p. 2). Temps. 16 Oct. (*CPR 1388–92* p. 121). D. 29 March 1404 (*Reg. Mascall* p. 94). Biog. ref.: *BRUO* III 1900–2; R. G. Davies, 'Trefnant, John (d. 1404)', *ODNB* <http://www. oxforddnb.com/view/article/41197>.

M. Robert Mascall O.Carm., DTh 1404–16

Lic. el. 12 Apr. 1404 (*CPR 1401–5* p. 385). Prov. 2 July (*CPL* V 583). Cons. 6 July (*Reg. Mascall* p. 6). Temps. 25 Sept (*CPR 1401–5* p. 421). Prof. of obed. 28 Sept. (Lamb., Reg. Arundel i fo. 28). D. 22 Dec. 1416 (Cant., *Reg. Chichele*

III 427). Biog. ref.: *BRUO* II 1239; R. G. Davies, 'Mascall, Robert (d. 1416)', *ODNB* <http://www.oxforddnb.com/view/article/18257>.

M. Edmund Lacy DTh 1417–20

Custody of temps. from 4 Jan. 1417 (*CPR 1416–22* p. 56). Lic. el. 21 Jan. (*ibid.*). Royal assent to el. 17 Feb. (*ibid.* p. 65). Conf. by abp. 31 March (Cant., *Reg. Chichele* I 33–4). Cons. 18 Apr. (*ibid.*; *Reg. Lacy H* p. 1). Prof. of obed. s.d. (Cant., *Reg. Chichele* I 35). Temps. 1 May (*CPR 1416–22* p. 104). Trans. to Exeter 1420. Also preb. of Hinton. Biog. ref.: *BRUO* II 1081–3; N. I. Orme, 'Lacy, Edmund (*c.*1370– 1455)', *ODNB* <http://www.oxforddnb.com/view/article/15846>.

M. Thomas Polton BCL 1420–1

Prov. 15 July 1420 (Cant., *Reg. Chichele* I 71). Cons. 21 July (*Eubel* I 274). Spirit. 7 Oct., prof. of obed. by proxy 4 Nov. (Cant., *Reg. Chichele* I 71–2). Temps. 9 Nov. (*CPR 1416–22* p. 304). Trans. to Chichester 1421. Biog. ref.: *BRUO* III 1494–5; M. Harvey, 'Polton, Thomas (d. 1433)', *ODNB* <http://www.oxforddnb.com/view/article/22482>.

Thomas Spofford OSB, SchTh 1421–48

Trans. from Rochester 18 Nov. 1421 (*Reg. Spofford* pp. 2–4). Cons. 24 May 1422 (*ibid.* pp. 5, 16–17). Temps. 25 May (*CPR 1416–22* p. 436). Prof. of obed. and spirit. 29 May (Cant., *Reg. Chichele* I 79). Abp.'s mand. to chapt. to enthr. 4 July 1423 (*ibid.* p. 37). After several attempts to res., res. by 4 Dec. 1448 (*Reg. Spofford* pp. ix, x, 251–4; *CPL* X p. 42). Biog. ref.: *BRUO* III 1744.

M. Richard Beauchamp DCnL 1448–50

Prov. 4 Dec. 1448 (*CPL* X 42; HCA 1814). Temps. 31 Jan. 1449 (*CPR 1446–52* p. 223). Prof. of obed. n.d. (Lamb., Reg Stafford fo. 31). Cons. 9 Feb. (*Reg. Beauchamp* p. 3). Enthr. 25 Apr. (*ibid.* p. 4). Trans. to Salisbury 1450. Biog. ref.: *BRUO* I 137–8; R. G. Davies, 'Beauchamp, Richard (d. 1481)', *ODNB* <http://www.oxforddnb.com/view/article/1839>.

M. Reginald Boulers OSB, DTh 1450–3

Prov. 18 Sept. 1450 (*Reg. Boulers* p. 1). Temps. 23 Dec. (*CPR 1446–52* p. 409). Lic. *alibi consecrari* 27 Jan. 1451 (Cant., Reg. S fo. 158b/186b). Cons. 8 Feb. (*Reg. Boulers* p. 1). Enthr. 2 Aug. (*ibid.* p. 11). Trans. to Coventry and Lichfield 1453. Biog. ref.: *BRUO* I 228–9; W. Smith, 'Boulers, Reginald (d. 1459)', *ODNB* <http://www.oxforddnb.com/view/article/50264>.

M. John Stanbury O.Carm., DTh 1453–74

Trans. from Bangor 7 Feb. 1453 (*Reg. Stanbury* p. 1; HCA 1456). Temps. 26 March (*CPR 1452–61* p. 48). Prof. of obed. 2 Apr. (Lamb., Reg. Kempe fos. 215b–16). Enthr. 25 Apr. (*Reg. Stanbury* pp. 6–7). D. 11 May 1474 (*BRUO* III 1755). Biog. ref.: *BRUO* III 1755; A. Rhydderch, 'Stanbury, John (d. 1494)', *ODNB* <http://www.oxforddnb.com/view/article/26228>.

M. Thomas Myllyng OSB, DTh 1474–92

Lic. el. 29 June 1474 (*CPR 1467–77* p. 448). Prov. 22 June (*CPL* XIII 887). Temps. 15 Aug. (*CPR 1467–77* p. 467). Lic. *alibi consecrari* s.d. (Cant., Reg. S fo. 70/266). Cons. 21 Aug. (*Reg. Myllyng* p. 1). D. by 12 Jan. 1492 (*ibid.* p. 144). Biog. ref.: *BRUO* II 1282–3; A. Rhydderch, 'Myllyng, Thomas (d. 1492)', *ODNB* <http://www.oxforddnb.com/view/article/18776>.

M. Edmund Audley DTh 1492–1502

Custody of temps. 11 March 1492 (*CPR 1485–94* p. 381). Trans. from Rochester by prov. 22 June (Cant., *Reg. Morton* I no. 40). Lic. el. 13 Nov. (*CPR 1485–94* p. 410). Temps. 26 Dec. (*ibid.* pp. 411–12). Trans. to Salisbury 1502. Also preb. of Colwall. Biog. ref.: *BRUO* I 75–6; J. Hughes, 'Audley, Edmund (*c.*1439–1524)', *ODNB* <http://www.oxforddnb.com/view/article/891>.

Adrian Castello 1502–4

Prov. 14 Feb. 1502 (*Eubel* II 163). Cons. by May 1502 (*RSA* p. 95). Oath by proxy n.d. (TNA, PROB 11/13). Trans. to Bath and Wells, prov. 2 Aug. 1504. Biog. ref.: T. F. Mayer, 'Castellesi, Adriano (*c.*1461–1521)', *ODNB* <http://www. oxforddnb.com/view/article/174>.

M. Richard Mayew DTh 1504–16

Prov. 9 Aug. 1504 (*Reg. Mayew* p. 3). Lic. *alibi consecrari* 24 Oct. (Cant., Reg. T fo. 35/455). Cons. 27 Oct. (*Reg. Mayew* p. 1). Temps. 1 Nov. (*CPR 1494–1509* p. 387). After enthr. by proxy received at cath. 15 Aug. 1505 (*Reg. Mayew* p. 6). D. 18 Apr. 1516 (*BRUO* II 1247). Biog. ref.: *BRUO* II 1247; D. G. Newcombe, 'Mayew, Richard (1439/40–1516)', *ODNB* <http://www.oxforddnb.com/view/article/68880>.

M. Charles Booth DCL 1516–35

Nominated by k. 22 Apr. 1516 (*Reg. Booth* p. 1). Custody of temps. 17 May (*ibid.*). Prov. 21 July (*L&P* II i no. 2199). Lic. *alibi consecrari* 22 Nov. (Lamb., Reg. Warham i fo. 19). Cons. 30 Nov. (*Reg. Booth* p. 1). Spirit. 1 Dec. (*ibid.* p. 10). Archdcn. of Canterbury's mand. to enthr. n.d. [Jan.] 1517, enthr. by proxy Jan. 1517 (HCA 7031/1 fo. 9v; *Reg. Booth* pp. 11–12). Temps. 19 Feb. 1519 (*ibid.* p. 21). D. 5 May 1535 (*ibid.* p. 301). Biog. ref.: *BRUC* p. 77; D. G. Newcombe, 'Booth, Charles (d. 1535)', *ODNB* <http://www.oxforddnb.com/view/article/42092>.

M. Edward Fox DTh 1535–8

Nominated by k. 20 Aug. 1535 and again by Thomas Cromwell 22 Aug. (HCA 2237; 7031/1 fo. 74). El. 25 Aug. (HCA 7031/1 fo. 74v). Royal assent 2 Sept. (*Foedera* VI ii 209). Temps. 7 Sept. (*L&P* IX i no. 729 (6)). Abp.'s conf. 15 Sept. (Lamb., Reg. Cranmer fo. 173). Cons. 26 Sept., spirit. 14 Oct. (*Reg. Booth* p. 361). D. 8 May 1538 (*ibid.* p. 381). Biog. ref.: A. A. Chibbi, 'Fox, Edward (1496–1538)', *ODNB* <http://www.oxforddnb.com/view/article/10027>.

M. Edmund Bonner DCL 1538–9

Lic. el. 5 Oct. 1538 (*Foedera* VI iv 18). El. 26 Oct. (HCA 7031/1 fo. 82). Royal assent 27 Nov. (*Foedera* VI iv 18). Abp.'s conf. 17 Dec. (Lamb., Reg. Cranmer fos.

217v–222v). Temps. 4 March (*Foedera* VI iv 19). El. bp. of London 20 Oct. 1539. Biog. ref.: *BRUO 1500–40* pp. 57–9; K. Carleton, 'Bonner, Edmund (d. 1569)', *ODNB* <http://www.oxforddnb.com/view/article/2850>.

M. John Skip DTh 1539–52

Warrant 11 Oct. 1539 for congé d'elire (no name); issued 13 Oct. (*L&P* XIV ii no. 435 (11)). El. 24 Oct. (HCA 7031/1 fo. 84v). Warrant 5 Nov. for royal assent; gr. 7 Nov.; assent signified to abp. 8 Nov. for conf. (*L&P* XIV ii nos. 619 (16), 619 (22); HRO, AL 19/14 fo. 1r–v; cf. Lamb., Reg. Cranmer fo. 249r, where 8 Nov. is assumed to have been the date of assent). Warrant 17 Nov. for temps.; gr. 18 Nov. (*L&P* XIV ii no. 619 (43); HCA 2236). Abp.'s conf. 20 Nov. (Lamb., Reg. Cranmer fos. 247v–254v; HRO, AL 19/14 fo. 1r). Cons. 23 Nov. (HRO, AL 19/14 fo. 1v). Archdcn. of Canterbury's mand. to enthr. 24 Nov.; appointed proctor 1 Dec.; enthr. by proxy 7 Dec. (HRO, AL 19/14 fos. 2r–3v). Spirit. gr. by k. 19 Dec. (HRO, AL 19/14 fos. 3v–4v). D. 28 March 1552 (HRO, AL 19/14 fo. 87v). Biog. ref.: D. G. Newcombe, 'Skip, John (d. 1552)', *ODNB* <http://www.oxforddnb.com/view/article/25691>.

DEANS

The endowment of the deanery was the manors of Breinton, Withington and Allensmore, the chap. of Preston, the rectories of Alansmore and Kingston, and portions of the chs. of Hampton Bishop, St Devereux, Tupsley, Prestbury, Sevenhampton, Portfield, Shelwick, Sugwas, Bromyard, Whitbourne, Eastnor, Colwall, Ledbury, Barton, Bishops Frome, Bosbury, Upton Bishop, Ross and Cradley and tithe in Lugg meadow, which was valued at 40m in 1294 and £38 6s 1½d in 1535 (*Reg. Swinfield* 305; *Valor* III 4).

John of Aigueblanche 1282–1320

After a lengthy dispute the curia awarded deanery to Aigueblanche 3–4 July 1282 (*Reg. Swinfield* pp. 318–26). Resident from 29 Sept. 1285 × 28 Sept. 1286 until d. (HCA R378–408). D. 13 Feb. × 20 March 1320 (*Ch. & Rec.* pp. 186–90). Also preb. of Bullinghope.

M. Stephen of Ledbury 1323–53
Baldwin Talbot 1343

Deanery vac. 9 May 1322 (HCA 2465). Prov. to deanery and preb. Bullinghope at k.'s request 16 Sept. 1323 to Ledbury; conf. of prov. 26 Jan. 1327 (*CPL* II 234, 255). Occ. 29 Sept. × 31 Dec. 1323 (HCA R412). Prov. and reservn. unnamed preb. to Talbot 12 Nov. 1343 (*CPP* p. 29). But Ledbury d. as dean by 17 Apr. 1353 (*Reg. Trillek* p. 387). Biog. ref.: Ledbury, *BRUO* II 1121.

M. Thomas Trillek 1353–61

Papal conf. of el. 6 Sept. 1353 but deanery vac. 1 Dec. (*CPP* p. 251; HCA 1932). Appointed after el. in ignorance of reservn. to pope 23 Jan. 1355 (*CPL* III 541). Occ. 30 May 1361 (HCA 992) but seems to have res. by 28 July and had done so by 23 Jan. 1363 (*CPR 1361–4* p. 44; *CPP* p. 398). Also preb. of Moreton Parva.

Biog. ref.: *BRUO* III 1906–8; D. Lepine, 'Trillek, Thomas (b. in or before 1312, d. 1372)', *ODNB* <http://www.oxforddnb.com/view/article/95196>.

William de Feriby 1361
M. William Birmingham DTh 1362–*c*.1377
M. John de Middleton DTh ?–1382

Royal gr. to Feriby 28 July 1361 (*CPR 1361–4* p. 44). Birmingham had Innocent VI's verbal promise of the deanery; prov. by Urban V 7 Apr., 21 Nov. 1362 and 23 Jan. 1363 (*CPP* pp. 385, 398–9; *L&G* p. 162). Birmingham occ. as dean 28 Feb. 1366 and *W. decanus* occ. from 29 Sept. × 31 Dec. 1372 until 29 Sept. × 31 Dec. 1377 (HCA 1811, R440–4). Middleton had reservn. of dig. 28 Jan. 1371 (*Lettres Gregoire XI* no. 9621). Exch. arranged by Middleton at the papal curia with Birmingham, when senile, for ch. of Berkeswell, Warwicks. (*Ch. & Rec.* pp. 240–1) but not recognized by bp. *J Decano* occ. 29 Sept. × 31 Dec. 1381, probably Middleton in view of subsequent judgt. (HCA R446). On d. of Birmingham, by 30 Apr. 1382 (Exeter, *Reg. Brantingham* p. 77), bp. coll. deanery to John Harold. Papal declaration 17 Oct. 1382 that Middleton's prov. was obtained by fraud, was invalid and that he should be removed (HCA 2892). Judgt. repeated 11 July 1383 by commissaries of the archdcn. of Canterbury (*Ch. & Rec.* pp. 239–46). Birmingham also preb. of Eigne and Moreton and Whaddon; Middleton also preb. of Cublington. Biog. ref.: Birmingham, *BRUO* I 177; Middleton, *BRUO* II 1276.

M. John Harold BCn&CL 1382–93

Coll. and papal prov. by 17 Oct. 1382 (HCA 2892; *Ch. & Rec.* pp. 239–46). A *J Decano* occ. 29 Sept. × 31 Dec. 1381, but probably Middleton. Harold occ. as dean 29 Sept. × 31 Dec. 1383 and subsequently until d. (HCA R448–56). D. 19 Oct. 1393 (*Reg. Trefnant* p. 56). Also preb. of Bullinghope, Moreton and Whaddon and Norton. Biog. ref.: *BRUO* II 877.

M. John Prophete 1393–1404

El. 7 Nov. 1393 (*Reg. Trefnant* pp. 52–8). Last occ. 29 Sept. × 31 Dec. 1401 (HCA R462). Res. by 12 Feb. 1404 (HCA 2898). Also preb. of Moreton Magna, Piona Parva and Warham. Biog. ref.: *BRUO* III 1521–3; R. G. Davies, 'Prophete, John (*c*.1350–1416)', *ODNB* <http://www.oxforddnb.com/view/article/37868>.

M. Thomas Felde DCL 1404–19

Bp.'s conf. of el. 12 Feb. 1404 (HCA 2898). D. 25 July × 13 Sept. 1419 (*Reg. Chichele* II 163–4; HCA 1457). Also preb. of Moreton Magna, Warham and Withington Parva. Biog. ref.: *BRUO* II 682–3.

M. John Baysham BCnL 1419–29/30

Bp.'s mand. adm. 13 Sept. 1419 (HCA 1457). Described as *nuper decanus* 29 Sept. 1429 × 28 Sept. 1430 (HCA R477). Also preb. of Moreton and Whaddon, Wellington and Withington Parva. Biog. ref.: *BRUO* I 135–6.

M. John Stanway BCL 1430–4

Occ. from 29 Sept. 1430 × 28 Sept. 1431 (HCA R478, 2086). D. 9 Aug. 1434 (*Reg. Spofford* p. 179). Also preb. of Cublington.

Henry Shelford 1434–46
   Bp.'s lic. el. 13 Aug. 1434; el. 20 Sept.; bp.'s conf. 26 Sept. (*Reg. Spofford* pp. 179–80). Last occ. 29 Sept. 1445 × 28 Sept. 1446 (HCA R484). Also preb. of Colwall. Biog. ref.: Richardson, *Chancery* pp. 80–1.

M. John Barowe BCn&CL 1446–62
   Occ. 29 Sept. 1446 × 28 Sept. 1447 (HCA R485). D. 6 Apr. 1462 (*Reg. Stanbury* p. 74). Also preb. of Withington Parva. Biog. ref.: *BRUO* I 116.

M. James Goldwell DCn&CL 1462–3
John ap Richard 1462–3
   Goldwell el. 14 June 1462 *per viam scrutinii* but as a result of armed violence by a faction ap Richard el. *per viam compromissi*. El. quashed by bp. 29 Jan. 1463 (*Reg. Stanbury* pp. 71–83). Goldwell also preb. of Wellington; Richard also treas. and preb. of Withington Parva. Biog. ref.: Goldwell, *BRUO* II 783–6; R. C. E. Hayes, 'Goldwell, James (d. 1499)', *ODNB* <http://www.oxforddnb.com/view/article/10926>.

M. Richard Pede DCnL 1463–81
   Coll. 14 March 1463 (*Reg. Stanbury* pp. 71–83). D. by 26 March 1481 (*Reg. Myllyng* p. 62). Also treas. and preb. of Hinton, Huntington and Moreton Magna. Biog. ref.: *BRUO* III 1449–50.

M. Thomas Chaundler DTh 1481–90
   Bp.'s conf. of el. 26 March 1481 (*Reg. Myllyng* p. 62). D. 2 Nov. 1490 (*Reg. Myllyng* p. 198; *Survey of Cath.* I 534). Also preb. of Gorwell and Overbury and Pratum Majus. Biog. ref.: *BRUO* I 398–9; J. Catto, 'Chaundler, Thomas (*c.*1417–90)', *ODNB* <http://www.oxforddnb.com/view/article/5200>.

M. Oliver King DCn&CL 1491
   El. 23 March 1491 (*Reg. Myllyng* p. 198). Res. 27 June (*ibid.* p. 136). Also preb. of Eigne. Biog. ref.: *BRUC* pp. 343–4; S. J. Gunn, 'King, Oliver (d. 1503)', *ODNB* <http://www.oxforddnb.com/view/article/15580>.

M. John Hervey BCnL 1491–1501
   Occ. 29 Sept. 1491 × 28 Sept. 1492 (HCA R529). D. 10 Aug. 1500 × 1 Feb. 1501 (Cant., Reg. F fos. 13r–14v). Also prec. and preb. of Putson Minor.

M. Reginald West 1503, 1507
   Occ. 30 Oct. 1503 (*Reg. Mayew* p. 10) and 11 May 1507 (*CPL* XVIII no. 732). May have res. by 5 July 1508 when res. preb. Pratum Minus (*Reg. Mayew* p. 275). Biog. ref.: *BRUO* III 2019.

M. Thomas Wolsey BTh ?–1512
   Occ. 4 June 1509 (*L&P* I i 245). Res. 3 Dec. 1512 (*Reg. Mayew* p. 148). Also preb. of Pratum Minus. Biog. ref.: *BRUO* III 2077–80; S. M. Jack, 'Wolsey, Thomas (1470/1–1530)', *ODNB* <http://www.oxforddnb.com/view/article/29854>.

M. Edmund Froucetur 1513–29

El. 21 Jan. 1513; bp.'s conf. 27 Jan. (*Reg. Mayew* pp. 149, 157–64). Instal. in person 17 Aug. × Nov. 1513 (HCA 7031/1 fo. 3v). D. 16 May 1529 (*Reg. Booth* p. 213). Also treas. and preb. of Colwall, Norton and Putson Major. Biog. ref.: *BRUO* II 732.

M. Gamaliel Clifton DCnL 1529–41

Royal nom. 24 Jan. 1529 as deanery likely to fall vac. soon (HCA 7031/1 fo. 47r–v) and again 4 June (the deanery by now being vac.) (*ibid.* fos. 47v–48r). El. 5 July; accepted el. by proxy 6 July; bp.'s conf. 21 July; instal. by proxy 22 July (*Reg. Booth* pp. 209–29; HCA 7031/1 fos. 47r–61r). Instal. again in person 14 Aug. 1530 (HCA 7031/1 fo. 65v). D. 29 Apr. 1541 (HRO, AL 19/14 fo. 24r). Also preb. of Colwall and Pratum Minus. Biog. ref.: *BRUC* p. 141.

PRECENTORS

The endowment of the precentorship was rents at Tupsley, the rectory of Walford, Herefs., the chap. of Ruardean, Glos., and portions of the chs. of Sevenhampton, Ross on Wye, Ledbury, Tupsley, Barton, Hampton Bishop, Shelwick, Bosbury, Whitbourne, Portfield, Bishops Frome, Bromyard, Upton Bishop, Sugwas, Cradley, Eastnor, Barton in Colwall and St Devereux, which was valued at 40m in 1294 and £21 19s 5d in 1535 (*Reg. Swinfield* p. 305; *Valor* III 8).

M. John de Swinfield 1294–1311

Coll. 21 Sept. 1294 (*Reg. Swinfield* p. 529). Last occ. 1 Jan. × 24 March 1311 (HCA R397). Also preb. of Putson Major. Biog. ref.: A. B. Emden, 'Additions and corrections to *A Biographical Register of the University of Oxford to 1500* no. 2', *Bodleian Library Record*, vii (1964) 160.

M. Richard de Havering 1311–41
M. John Ewe or **Oo of Oxford** 1330
M. John de Ashton 1330

Havering first occ. as prec. 29 Sept. × 1 Jan. 1311 (HCA R399). Royal gr. to Ewe 13 March 1330 and 1 May to Ashton (*CPR 1327–30* pp. 498, 500, 522). Havering occ. 29 Sept. × 31 Dec. 1330 to 29 Sept. × 31 Dec. 1338 (HCA R417–24). Revocation of gr. to Ewe 10 Dec. 1330 and Havering's estate ratif. (*CPR 1330–4* p. 25). Havering d. by 29 Jan. 1341 (Lichfield Joint RO, Reg. Northburgh fo. 114v). Ewe also treas. and preb. of Colwall; Havering also preb. of Putson Minor. Biog. ref.: Havering, *BRUO* III 2181–2; Ewe, *BRUO* II 1399.

M. Giles de Stamford 1341

By coll., possibly by 1 Jan. × 24 March 1341 when occ. as can. (HCA R426); ordered by pope to res. 22 July 1341 (*CPL* II 551). Also preb. of Putson Minor.

M. Thomas of Winchester 1342–9

Prov. 14 Oct. 1342 (*CPP* p. 10). Exch. 20 Nov. 1349 with Walter Elveden for archdcnry. of Sudbury (*Reg. Trillek* p. 406; Norwich, *The Register of William*

Bateman, Bishop of Norwich 1344–1355, ed. P. E. Pobst (2 vols., Canterbury and York Soc., lxxxxiv, xc, 1996–2000), II no. 1263).

M. Walter Elveden DCL 1349–58
By exch. Nov. 1349. Exch. 10 Dec. 1358 with Ralph of Coggeshall for ch. of Shropham, Norf. (*Reg. Trillek* p. 409). Biog. ref.: *BRUC* p. 210.

Ralph of Coggeshall 1358–61
By exch. Dec. 1358. D. by 8 March 1361 (*CPR 1358–61* p. 566).

Henry Snaith 1361
Henry de Bernyngton 1361
Hugh Heremyte 1361–3
Royal gr. to Snaith 8 March 1361 (*CPR 1358–61* p. 566), to Bernyngton 13 Oct. (*CPR 1361–4* p. 88) and to Heremyte 10 Nov. (*ibid.* p. 108). Heremyte gained possession and exch. 8 June 1363 with William Outy for a preb. in St Stephen's Westminster (*ibid.* p. 345). Biog. ref.: Snaith, A. H. Thompson, 'Pluralism in the medieval church; with notes on pluralists in the diocese of Lincoln, 1366', *Associated Architectural and Archaeological Reports and Papers*, xxxv (1919–20) 239–40.

William Outy 1363–4
By exch. June 1363. Exch. 6 Aug. 1364 with William Borstall for ch. of Whittington, Glos. (*Reg. L. Charlton* p. 71).

William Borstall 1364–6
By exch. Aug. 1364. Archdcn. of Shropshire 1366, probably by exch. with Henry Shipton (*Reg. L. Charlton* p. 35; Cant., *Reg. Langham* pp. 41, 47). Also preb. of Bartonsham. Biog. ref.: McDermid, *Beverley Fasti*, pp. 72–3.

M. Henry de Shipton 1366–83
By exch. 1366. Occ 11 July 1383 (HCA 2893); last occ. as can. and probably prec. 24 June × 28 Sept. 1383 (HCA R447). Also treas., archdcn. of Shropshire and preb. of Hunderton and Putson Minor.

M. Walter of Ramsbury BTh 1384–1406
First occ. as can. and probably prec. 1 Jan. × 24 March 1384 (HCA R448). D. by 17 Nov. 1406 (*Reg. Mascall* p. 169). Also preb. of Wellington. Biog. ref.: *BRUO* III 1544–5.

Henry Myle 1406–7
Coll. 17 Nov. 1406; instal. by proxy 15 Dec. (*Reg. Mascall* p. 169). Exch. 9 July 1407 with Richard Talbot for ch. St Laurence Ludlow (*ibid.* p. 183). Also preb. of Wellington.

M. Richard Talbot 1407–12
By exch. July 1407. Res. by 26 Oct. 1412 (*Reg. Mascall* p. 178). Also preb. of Putson Major. Biog. ref.: *BRUO* III 1545–6; E. Matthew, 'Talbot, Richard (d. 1449)', *ODNB* <http://www.oxforddnb.com/view/article/26939>.

M. Fulk Stafford BCL 1412–13

Coll. 26 Oct. 1412 (*Reg. Mascall* p. 178). D. by 13 Feb. 1413 (Exeter, *The Register of Edmund Stafford, Bishop of Exeter, 1395–1419: and Index and Abstract of its Contents*, ed. F. C. Hingeston-Randolph (1886) p. 205). Biog. ref.: *BRUO* III 1750.

M. Nicholas Colnet MA 1413

Coll. 3 March 1413 (*Reg. Mascall* p. 178). Res. by 12 Dec. (*ibid.* p. 179). Biog. ref.: *BRUO* I 149.

Robert Felton 1413–16

Coll. 12 Dec. 1413 (*Reg. Mascall* p. 179). Res. by 7 March 1416 (*ibid.* p. 89). Also preb. of Gorwell and Overbury.

M. John Bridbroke LicCnL 1416–32

Coll. 29 July 1416 (*Reg. Mascall* p. 182). Exch. 9 Aug. 1432 with William Lochard for a preb. in St George's chap. Windsor (*Reg. Spofford* p. 369). Also preb. of Colwall. Biog. ref.: *BRUC* pp. 92–3.

William Lochard 1432–8

By exch. Aug. 1432. D. 24 Nov. 1438 m.i. Hereford cath. (*Survey of Cath.* I 539). Also preb. of Bullinghope.

William Middleham ?–1463

Occ. 2 Sept. 1443 (*Reg. Spofford* p. 251). D. 28 July × 4 Dec. 1463 (*Records of Convocation*, ed. G. Bray (20 vols., Church of England Record Soc., Woodbridge 2005–6) VI 165; *Reg. Stanbury* p. 179). Also treas. and preb. of Bullinghope and Eigne.

M. John Baily BCL 1463–79

Coll. 23 Dec. 1463 (*Reg. Stanbury* p. 179). D. 5 July × 8 Sept. 1479 (HCA R369; *Reg. Myllyng* p. 189). Also preb. of Episcopi, Ewithington and Warham. Biog. ref.: *BRUO* I 91.

M. Thomas Downe 1479–89

Coll. 8 Sept. 1479 (*Reg. Myllyng* p. 189). D. 26 March 1489 (*ibid.* p. 197; *Survey of Cath.* I 540). Also preb. of Episcopi and Wellington.

M. John Hervey BCnL 1489–91

Coll. 3 Apr. 1489 (*Reg. Myllyng* p. 197). Dean 1491. Also preb. of Putson Minor.

M. Robert Kent DTh ?–1515

Occ. as can. 29 Sept. 1486 × 28 Sept. 1487 (HCA R524), probably prec. from 1491. Occ. as prec. 29 Sept. 1496 × 28 Sept. 1497 (HCA 4328). D. 4 Aug. × 15 Oct. 1515 (TNA, PROB 11/18). Also preb. of Episcopi. Biog. ref.: *BRUO* II 1037.

M. William Porter BTh 1515–24
   Coll. 21 Oct. 1515 (*Reg. Mayew* p. 284). Instal. Nov. (HCA 7031/1 fo. 7v). D. 5 Nov. 1524 (*Reg. Booth* p. 338; *Survey of Cath.* I 540). Also preb. of Episcopi. Biog. ref.: *BRUO* III 1503.

M. Rowland Philippes LicTh 1524–31
   Coll. 6 Nov. 1524 (*Reg. Booth* p. 338). Instal. in person 17 Nov. (HCA 7031/1 fo. 36r). Res. by 7 Apr. 1531 (*Reg. Booth* p. 345). Also preb. of Episcopi. Biog. ref.: *BRUO* III 1477–8; J. P. D. Cooper, 'Philipps, Rowland (1467/8–1538?)', *ODNB* <http://www.oxforddnb.com/view/article/22132>.

M. Thomas Parker DCnL 1531–8
   Coll. 7 Apr. 1531 (*Reg. Booth* p. 345). Instal. s.d. (HCA 7031/1 fo. 66v). D. 22 Sept. 1538 (*L&P* XIII no. 491 (19)). Also preb. of Episcopi and Huntington. Biog. ref.: *BRUO 1500–40* p. 433.

M. Richard Benese BCnL 1538–47
   Royal gr. *sede vacante* 30 Oct. 1538; instal. 11 Nov. (HCA 7031/1 fo. 82r). Chancery warrant 23 Dec. for further royal gr. *sede vacante*; letter patent issued 24 Dec. (*L&P* XIII ii no. 1182 (32); TNA, C 82/747).[1] D. 3 Nov. 1546 × 7 Jan. 1547 (TNA, PROB 11/31; HRO, AL 19/14 fo. 68v). Biog. ref.: *BRUO 1500–40* pp. 41–2; J. Hughes, 'Benese, Richard (d. 1547)', *ODNB* <http://www.oxforddnb.com/view/article/2088>.

CHANCELLORS

The endowment of the chancellorship was the rectory of Little Hereford with the chap. of Ashford Carbonell, which was valued at 30m in 1294 and £14 3s 4d in 1535 (*Reg. Swinfield* p. 305; *Valor* III 8); Little Hereford was valued at £20 in 1291 (*Taxatio* p. 157a).

M. Robert of Gloucester or **le Wyse** DCnL 1299–1322
   Coll. 16 Sept. 1299 (*Reg. Swinfield* p. 531). D. by 31 Jan. 1322 (*Reg. Orleton* p. 387). Also preb. of Hunderton and Huntington. Biog. ref.: *BRUO* II 773–4.

M. Thomas Orleton 1322–33
   Coll. 31 Jan. 1322 (*Reg. Orleton* p. 387). Last occ. 25 March × 23 June 1333 (HCA R418). Also held unidentified preb.

Robert Wynferthing ?–1343
   Expect. preb. and dig. 23 Oct. 1331 (*Lettres Jean XXII* no. 55502). Occ. 1 Aug. 1334 (*CPR 1334–8* p. 3). Res. 31 Jan. 1343 (*CPP* p. 13).

---

[1] This may have been intended as a reissue of the previous gr., as Edmund Bonner had been conf. to the bpc. on 17 Dec. and the see was no longer vac.

M. Richard de Wymundeswold DCL 1343–5
John de Charnele 1344
   Prov. to Wymundeswold 10 Feb. 1343 (*CPP* p. 13). Royal gr. to Charnele 15 Sept. 1344 and prohibns. in his favour 16 Sept. (*CPR 1343–5* pp. 339, 349; HCA 2254). Called chanc. 21 Sept. 1344 (HCA 2467). But Wymundeswold res. this dig. by 26 June 1345 (*CPL* III 183). Biog. ref.: Wymundeswold, *BRUC* pp. 659–60.

M. John Ambresbury 1345–9
   Prov. 26 June 1345 (*CPL* III 183). D. by 23 June 1349 (*Reg. Trillek* p. 376).

Thomas Hacluit 1349–75
   Coll. 23 June 1349 (*Reg. Trillek* p. 376). Papal conf. 16 Oct. (*CPP* p. 180). Occ. 25 March × 23 June 1374 and d. by 22 Feb. 1375 (HCA R441; *Reg. Gilbert* p. 107; *L&G* p. 496). Also preb. of Hampton.

M. Nicholas Hereford MA 1375
M. Betrand Lagier of Figeac OFM, DTh, card. bp. of Ostia ?–1381
Andreas Bontempi card. pr. of SS. Marcellinus et Petrus 1381–?
   Hereford gr. expect. of preb. and dig. 26 March 1371 (*L&G* p. 424; *Lettres Gregoire XI* no. 9694). Prov. to Lagier 23 Sept. 1372 but did not gain possession (*L&G* p. 496). Hereford gained temporary possession and had papal conf. 22 Feb. 1375 (*ibid.*; *Reg. Gilbert* p. 106). His title was questioned by bp. on the grounds that the patronage of the chancellorship belonged to the k. because of the episcopal vac. caused by Courtenay's transl. 12 Sept. 1375 (*Reg. Gilbert* p. 106). Royal gr. to Hereford 20 Feb. 1377 but ineffective (*CPR 1374–7* p. 426; *Ch. & Rec.* p. 238). On 30 Aug. 1381 the property of the chancellorship was in the possession of Sir Peter de la Mare and on 20 Oct. 1387 it was said to have been in his hands for twelve years (*CCR 1381–5* p. 16; *Reg. Gilbert* p. 107). Lagier depriv. of this dig. by the pope by 18 Aug. 1381; royal gr. to Bontempi s.d. (*CPR 1377–81* p. 615). Hereford also treas. and preb. of Pratum Majus and Minus, and Putson Minor; Lagier also claimed preb. of Gorwell and Overbury. Biog. ref.: Hereford, *BRUO* II 913–15; Lagier, C. Berton, *Dictionnaire des cardinaux* (Paris, 1857) pp. 117–18; Bontempi, *Dictionnaire d'histoire et de géographie ecclésiastiques* (Paris, 1912–) IX 1124.

John de Nottingham 1387–9
   Royal gr. 27 Apr. 1387 (*CPR 1385–9* p. 299). Inquiry by bp. into the history of the chancellorship since 1375, 15 June 1387 (*Reg. Gilbert* pp. 105–7). Bp. gr. Nottingham the income of the chancellorship during vac. to repair the chanc.'s house 22 Oct. 1387 (HCA 2895). Nottingham exch. chancellorship, preb. Gaia Major in Lichfield and preb. in St George's Chapel Windsor *c.* 6 Jan. 1389 with Thomas Hanley for ch. of Cottingham, Yorks. (*CPR 1385–9* p. 538; Lichfield, Reg. Scrope fo. 34v). Biog. ref.: McDermid, *Beverley Fasti* p. 28.

Thomas Hanley 1389–?
John Ashwell 1389
   Hanley became chanc. by exch. Jan. 1389. Exch. 6 March with Ashwell for ch. of Thurcaston, Leics. (*CPR 1388–92* p. 22). This exch. apparently ineffective as

Hanley's estate ratif. 24 Jan. 1391 (*ibid.* p. 290). Bp.'s mand. inquiry into Hanley's right 23 Apr. 1392 (HCA 2457).

M. Nicholas Hereford (again) 1394–7
Royal gr. 16 Feb. 1394 (*CPR 1391–6* p. 372). Treas. 1397. Biog. ref.: *BRUO* II 913–15.

Thomas Hanley (again) ?–1417
Occ. 31 Oct. 1399 (*CPR 1399–1401* p. 136). Res. by 20 Oct. 1417 (*Reg. Lacy H* p. 113).

Richard Proctor 1417–25
Coll. 20 Oct. 1417 (*Reg. Lacy H* p. 113). Res. 10 May 1425 (*Reg. Spofford* p. 87).

M. John Castell BCL 1425–8
Coll. 7 July 1425 (*Reg. Spofford* p. 352). Exch. with Richard Proctor 2 Dec. 1428 for ch. of St Clement Danes, London (London, GL MS. 9531/5 fo. 23v). Also preb. of Episcopi. Biog. ref.: *BRUO* I 368.

Richard Proctor (again) 1428–?
By exch. Dec. 1428.

M. Richard Rotherham DTh ?1435, 1441, 1447
Occ. 12 Dec. 1435, 5 Feb. 1441 (*Reg. Spofford* pp. 207, 241) and 29 Sept. 1446 × 28 Sept. 1447 (HCA 2370). Probably res. or exch. in 1448 after he became resident at Exeter (Devon RO, Exeter Cathedral Archives, D&C 3759 fo. 60v). Also treas. and preb. of Episcopi and Huntington. Biog. ref.: *BRUO* III 1953.

M. John Dylew or **Dellow** BCn&CL ?–1460
Occ. 8 Sept. × 1 Dec. 1449 (*Reg. Beauchamp* pp. 7–8). D. by 6 July 1460 (*Reg. Stanbury* p. 176). Also preb. of Episcopi and unidentified preb. Biog. ref.: *BRUO* I 566–7.

M. John Asheby 1460–4
Coll. 6 July 1460 (*Reg. Stanbury* p. 176). D. by 16 Aug. 1464 (*ibid.* p. 180). Also treas. and preb. of Cublington and Moreton Parva.

M. Robert Geffrey MA 1464–72
Coll. 16 Aug. 1464 (*Reg. Stanbury* p. 180). Exch. 24 March 1472 with Thomas Yone for archdcnry. of Shropshire (*ibid.* p. 188). Also treas., archdcn. of Hereford and preb. of Inkberrow and Preston. Biog. ref.: *BRUO* II 753–4.

M. Thomas Yone BCnL 1472
By exch. March 1472. D. by 24 Nov. (*Reg. Stanbury* p. 188). Also archdcn. of Shropshire and preb. of Pratum Minus. Biog. ref.: *BRUO* III 2134.

M. Simon Tawre BCnL 1472–6

Coll. 24 Nov. 1472 (*Reg. Stanbury* p. 188). D. by 8 Oct. 1476 (*Reg. Myllyng* p. 187). Also preb. of Cublington and Warham. Biog. ref.: *BRUO* III 1850.

M. John Arundel BTh 1476–81

Coll. 8 Oct. 1476 (*Reg. Myllyng* p. 187). Res. by 5 March 1481 (*ibid.* p. 191). Also treas. and preb. of Cublington. Biog. ref.: *BRUO* I 50–1; N. I. Orme, 'Arundel, John (*c.*1435–1503)', *ODNB* <http://www.oxforddnb.com/view/article/720>.

M. Ralph Heathcott BCnL 1481–7

Coll. 5 March 1481 (*Reg. Myllyng* p. 191). Res. by 12 Dec. 1487 (*ibid.* p. 196). Biog. ref.: *BRUO* II 923.

M. Samson Aleyn BCL 1487–94

Coll. 12 Dec. 1487 (*Reg. Myllyng* p. 196). D. by Oct 1494 (*BRUO* I 23). Biog. ref.: *BRUO* I 23.

M. James Bromwich BCnL ?–1524

First occ. as can. and possibly chanc. 29 Sept. 1494 × 28 Sept. 1495 (HCA R531). Occ. as chanc. in Mayew's episcopate (1504 × 16) (*Reg. Mayew* pp. 39, 234). D. 3 Feb. × 16 April 1524 (HCA 7031/1 fo. 34; *Reg. Booth* p. 337). Also preb. of Church Withington. Biog. ref.: *BRUO* I 277.

M. William Hulle MA 1524–43

Coll. 16 Apr. 1524 (*Reg. Booth* p. 337). Instal. 30 Apr. (HCA 7031/1 fo. 35r). D. 9 × 13 Aug. 1543 (TNA, PROB 11/30; HRO, AL 19/14 fo. 54v). Also preb. of Putson Major. Biog. ref.: *BRUO 1500–40* p. 684.

TREASURERS

The endowment of the treasurership was rents in Breinton, Hereford and Walford, the rectories of Bockleton, Worcs., and Bartonsham, income from the shrine of St Thomas Cantilupe in Hereford cath. and, from 1525, St Ethelbert's Hospital Hereford, which was valued at 10m in 1294 and £15 8s in 1535 (*Reg. Swinfield* p. 305; *Valor* III 8).

M. Roger of Sevenoaks 1294–1300

Coll. 21 Sept. 1294 (*Reg. Swinfield* pp. 328, 529). D. by 15 Jan. 1300 (*ibid.* p. 531). Also preb. of Cublington.

M. Roger of Canterbury 1300–3

Coll. 15 Jan. 1300 (*Reg. Swinfield* p. 531). D. by 1 June 1303 (*ibid.* p. 534). Also archdcn. of Shropshire and preb. of Hinton, Preston and Wellington.

M. William Gaye or **de la Gare** 1303–4

Coll. 1 June 1303 (*Reg. Swinfield* p. 534). D. by 24 March 1304 (*ibid.* p. 535). Also preb. of Nonnington.

Nicholas of Reigate 1304–8
   Coll. 24 March 1304 (*Reg. Swinfield* p. 535). D. by 6 Apr. 1308 (*ibid.* p. 538). Also preb. of Wellington.

John of Kempsey 1308–17
   Coll. 6 Apr. 1308 (*Reg. Swinfield* p. 538). D. 9 × 26 May 1317 (HCA 1028, 2880). Also preb. of Colwall and Moreton Parva.

Thomas of Pembridge 1317–29
   Royal gr. 18 May 1317 (*CPR 1313–17* p. 651). D. by 24 Oct. 1329 (*Reg. T. Charlton* p. 76). Also preb. of Colwall.

M. John Ewe or **Oo of Oxford** 1329–?
   Coll. 24 Oct. 1329 (*Reg. T. Charlton* p. 76). Also prec. and preb. of Colwall. Biog. ref.: *BRUO* II 1399.

John de la Chambre 1331–3
M. Thomas de Boleie 1331–3
   Inquiry ordered 5 Apr. 1331 into Boleie's claim to treasurership held by Chambre (*Reg. T. Charlton* p. 7). Prov. of can. and treasurership to Chambre 23 June 1331 (*CPL* II 346). Coll. to Boleie 17 March 1333 (*ibid.* p. 77) but Chambre res. it 22 Dec. (*ibid.* p. 78). Chambre also preb. of Inkberrow. Biog. ref.: Chambre, *Hemingby's Register* pp. 189–90.

M. Henry de Shipton 1333–?
   Coll. 22 Dec 1333 (*Reg. T. Charlton* p. 78). Occ. 21 May 1334 (*ibid.* p. 144). Archdcn. Shropshire by 1346. Also prec. and preb. of Hunderton and Putson Minor.

M. Richard Sydenhale ?–1348
   Occ. as can. and possibly treas. 1 Jan. × 24 March 1339 (HCA R424). Exch. this dig. and preb. of Pratum Majus by 2 Dec. 1348 with John Boter for ch. Staunton-on-Wye, Herefs. (*Reg. Trillek* pp. 40, 406). Also archdcn. of Shropshire.

John Boter 1348–67
   By exch. Dec. 1348. Exch. 27 Nov. 1367 with Roger Mey for ch. of Whittington, Glos. (*Reg. L. Charlton* p. 72). Also preb. of Pratum Majus.

Roger Mey 1367–8
   By exch. Nov. 1367. Exch. 29 June 1368 with Robert Upcote for vic. of Credenhill, Herefs. (*Reg. L. Charlton* p. 72).

Robert Upcote 1368–77
John of Cricklade 1375
   Upcote treas. by exch. June 1368. Exch. 29 Jan 1375 with Cricklade for ch. of Withington, Herefs. (*CPR 1374–7* p. 69) but ineffective. Upcote exch. treasurership 21 March 1377 with Robert Jones for ch. of Eastleach Martin, Worcs. dioc. (*Reg. Gilbert* p. 115).

Robert Jones 1377–?

By exch. March 1377. Occ. 23 Dec. 1385 (*Reg. Gilbert* p. 87).

M. Nicholas Hereford DTh 1397–1417

Coll. 30 March 1397 (*Reg. Trefnant* p. 181). Res. 2 Nov. 1417 (*Reg. Lacy H* p. 113). Also chanc. and preb. of Pratum Majus and Minus and Putson Minor. Biog. ref.: *BRUO* II 913–15.

William Cave 1417–?
Richard Northop 1417–?

Coll. to Cave 6 Nov. 1417. Another contemporary hand has inserted the name of Northop in this entry in the reg. (perhaps in error?) (HRO, AL/19/8 fo. 2v; *Reg. Lacy H* p. 113). Cave also preb. of Putson Major.

M. Richard Rotherham DTh ?–1434

Occ. 27 Feb. 1433 (*Reg. Spofford* p. 152). Said to have held treasurership for 'sometime' 18 Sept. 1433 (*CPL* VIII 456). Res. 27 June 1434 (*Reg. Spofford* p. 359) but called treas., instead of chanc., 12 Oct. 1446 (*CPL* VIII 311). Also chanc. and preb. of Episcopi and Huntington. Biog. ref.: *BRUO* III 1593.

William Middleham 1434–?

Coll. 26 June 1434 (*Reg. Spofford* p. 359). Occ. 12 Dec. 1435 (*ibid.* p. 207). Prec. by Sept. 1443. Also preb. of Bullinghope and Eigne.

Thomas Wassayle ?–1443

Res. this dig. by 18 Nov. 1443 (*Reg. Spofford* p. 365).

M. Richard Rudhale DCnL 1443–6

Coll. 18 Nov. 1443 (*Reg. Spofford* p. 365). Bp.'s mand. adm. s.d. (HCA 2791). Archdcn. of Hereford 1446. Also preb. of Bullinghope and Huntington. Biog. ref.: *BRUO* III 1603.

M. John Asheby 1446–60

Coll. 4 Aug. 1446 (*Reg. Spofford* p. 366). Chanc. 1464. Also preb. of Cublington and Moreton Parva.

M. Richard Pede DCnL 1460–?

Coll. 6 July 1460 *in commendam* for six months (*Reg. Stanbury* p. 176). Also dean and preb. of Hinton, Huntington and Moreton Magna. Biog. ref.: *BRUO* II 1449–50.

John ap Richard ?–1463

Occ. 14 June 1462 (*Reg. Stanbury* p. 75). D. by 19 March 1463 (*ibid.* p. 178). Also el. dean and preb. of Withington Parva.

M. Robert Geffrey MA 1463–4

Coll. 19 March 1463 (*Reg. Stanbury* p. 178). Chanc. 1464. Also archdcn. of Hereford and Shropshire and preb. of Inkberrow and Preston. Biog. ref.: *BRUO* II 753–4.

M. John Arundel BTh 1464–76
Coll. 22 Aug. 1464 (*Reg. Stanbury* p. 180). Chanc. 1476. Also preb. of Cublington. Biog. ref.: *BRUO* I 50–1; N. I. Orme, 'Arundel, John (*c*.1435–1503)', *ODNB* <http://www.oxforddnb.com/view/article/720>.

Simon Stalworth or **Massingham** ?–1477
Res. this dig. by 27 Oct. 1477 (*Reg. Myllyng* p. 188). Biog. ref.: *BRUO* III 1753.

M. Adrian de Bardis 1477–86
Coll. 27 Oct. 1477 (*Reg. Myllyng* p. 188). Res. by 14 Dec. 1486 (*ibid.* p. 195). Also preb. of Moreton and Whaddon. Biog. ref.: *BRUC* p. 36.

M. Robert Sherborne BM 1486–?
Coll. 14 Dec. 1486 (*Reg. Myllyng* p. 195). Occ. 20 Oct. 1492 (Cant., *Reg. Morton* II no. 77). Biog. ref.: *BRUO* III 1685–7; C. Harper-Bill, 'Sherborne, Robert (*c*. 1454–1536)', *ODNB* <http://www.oxforddnb.com/view/article/25357>.

M. Owen Pole DCnL ?–1509
Occ. 14 Jan. 1496 and 16 Jan. 1503 (*CPL* XVI no. 624; HCA 7031/1 fo. 173). D. 10 × 18 Dec. 1509 (TNA, PROB 11/16; *Reg. Mayew* p. 277). Also preb. of Putson Major and unidentified preb. Biog. ref.: *BRUO* III 1491.

M. John Wardroper BCn&CL ?–1511
Occ. 10 March 1511 (*Reg. Mayew* p. 39). Res. by 22 July (*ibid.* p. 279). Also archdcn. of Shropshire and preb. of Bartonsham. Biog. ref.: *BRUO* III 1985.

M. Richard Judde BCnL 1511–12
Coll. 22 July 1511 (*Reg. Mayew* p. 279). D. 12 May 1512 (*ibid.* p. 182). Also preb. of Bullinghope.

M. Edmund Frouceter DTh 1512–13
Coll. 1 July 1512 (*Reg. Mayew* p. 280). Instal. 14 Aug. (HCA 7031/1 fo. 1r). Dean 1513. Also preb. of Colwall, Norton and Putson Major. Biog. ref.: *BRUO* II 732.

M. William Goberd BA 1513–15
Coll. 22 Feb. 1513 (*Reg. Mayew* p. 281). Instal. 12 March (HCA 7031/1 fo. 3r). Archdcn. of Shropshire 1515. Also preb. of Moreton and Whaddon and Piona Parva. Biog. ref.: *BRUO 1500–40* p. 236.

M. Henry Martin BCn&CL 1515–16
Instal. 22 Sept. 1515 (HCA 7031/1 fo. 7). Archdcn. of Shropshire 1516. Also preb. of Gorwell and Overbury, Inkberrow, Norton, Warham and Withington Parva. Biog. ref.: *BRUO* II 1234.

M. Hugh Pole MA 1516–19
    Coll. 13 Apr. 1516 (*Reg. Mayew* p. 284). Res. by 5 Jan. 1519 (*Reg. Booth* p. 332). Also preb. of Gorwell and Overbury, Hinton, Moreton and Whaddon and Norton. Biog. ref.: *BRUO* II 1490.

M. William Burghill DCnL 1519–26
    Coll. 5 Jan 1519 (*Reg. Booth* p. 332). D. 23 Aug. 1526 (*ibid.* p. 339; HCA 7031/1 fo. 38r). Also preb. of Bartonsham and Piona Parva. Biog. ref.: *BRUO 1500–40* p. 85.

M. Roger Brayne BCnL 1526–7
    Coll. 6 Sept. 1526 (*Reg. Booth* p. 339). Instal. 7 Sept. (HCA 7031/1 fo. 38r). D. by 7 March 1527 (*Reg. Booth* p. 340). Also preb. of Pratum Majus and Warham. Biog. ref.: *BRUO* I 255–6.

M. Nicholas Walwen 1527–45
    Coll. 10 March 1527 (*Reg. Booth* p. 340). D. 15 Dec. 1544 × 23 May 1545 (HCA 7031/1 fo. 91v; HRO, AL 19/14 fo. 61v). Also preb. of Eigne and Moreton Parva. Biog. ref.: *BRUO 1500–40* p. 707.

ARCHDEACONS OF HEREFORD

The income of the archdcn. was derived entirely from spirit. which in 1535 were valued at £41 17s 11d (*Valor* III 6–7).

M. Richard of Hertford 1287–1303
    Coll. 21 Nov. 1287 (*Reg. Swinfield* p. 527). D. by 1 June 1303 (*ibid.* p. 535). Also preb. of Withington Parva.

M. Henry de Shorne DCL 1303–18
    Coll. 1 June 1303 (*Reg. Swinfield* p. 527). Res. 13 Feb. 1318 (*Reg. Orleton* p. 60). Also preb. of Warham. Biog. ref.: *BRUO* III 1696.

M. Thomas Chaundos senior 1318–32
    Mand. to assign vac. archdcnry. void by cession of Shorne who held it as a pluralist without papal dispensation 18 July 1318 (*CPL* II 178). Occ. from 29 Sept. × 31 Dec. 1319 until 29 Sept. × 31 Dec. 1332 (HCA R408–18). D. by 3 Jan. 1333 (*Calendar of Inquisitions Post Mortem* VII no. 492). Also preb. of Bartonsham, Eigne and unidentified preb.

John de Barton 1333–?
    Coll. 5 March 1333 (*Reg. T. Charlton* p. 78). Occ. 29 Sept. 1335 when gr. canonical house, as archdcn.? (*ibid.* p. 79). Also held unidentified preb.

M. William of Sheynton BCL ?1338–66
    W. Arch occ. 25 March × 23 June 1338 (HCA R423). D. 20 Dec. 1366 (*Calendar of Inquisitions Post Mortem* XII no. 168). Also preb. of Cublington.

M. Roger Sutton DCL 1367
M. John of Bedwardine or **Smythes** ?1369–79
Prov. to Sutton 12 Aug. 1367 when vac. but ineffective (*L&G* p. 350). Bedwardine occ. 26 March 1369 (*Reg. L. Charlton* p. 69). *J Archidiacono* last occ. 24 June × 28 Sept. 1378 (HCA R444a). Res. 2 Apr. 1379 (*Reg. Gilbert* p. 6). Bedwardine also preb. of Bullinghope; Sutton also preb. of Eigne and Moreton and Whaddon. Biog. ref.: Sutton, *BRUC* p. 568.

Richard Kingston ?1380–1405
M. Richard Tissington 1379–80
Tissington occ. 24 June × 28 Sept. 1379 and 29 Sept. × 31 Dec. 1379 (HCA R444a–445). Kingston, called archdcn., appealed to papal see 25 Feb. 1380 against Tissington's claim (HCA 2891). Kingston called archdcn. 11 July 1383 (HCA 2893). Royal gr. to Kingston 26 July 1389 (*CPR 1388–92* p. 87). Res. by 31 Jan. 1405 (HRO, AL/19/6 fo. 1v). Kingston also preb. of Bullinghope, Cublington and Norton. Biog. ref.: Kingston, McDermid, *Beverley Fasti* pp. 64–5.

M. John Loveney 1405–17
Coll. 31 Jan. 1405 (HRO, AL/19/6 fo.1v). Exch. 5 May 1417 with John Hereford for archdcnry. of Shropshire (*Reg. Lacy H* pp. 119, 120). Also preb. of Withington Parva.

M. John Hereford or **Carpenter** BCnL 1417–24
By exch. May 1417. Res. by 21 July 1424 (*Reg. Spofford* pp. 52, 352). Also archdcn. of Shropshire and preb. of Nonnington.

M. John Barowe BCn&CL 1424–46
Coll. 21 July 1424 (*Reg. Spofford* p. 352). Exch. 10 July 1446 with Richard Rudhale for ch. Birdbrook, Essex (*ibid.* p. 370). Biog. ref.: *BRUO* I 116.

M. Richard Rudhale DCnL 1446–76
By exch. July 1446. D. 16 May × 20 July 1476 (TNA, PROB 11/6). Also treas. and preb. of Bullinghope and Huntington. Biog. ref.: *BRUO* III 1603.

M. Richard Martyn BCnL ?–1483
Occ. 25 July 1478 (*Reg. Myllyng* p. 202). Bp. of St Davids 1482 but had papal dispensation 26 Apr. 1482 to retain archdcnry. and preb. Moreton Magna (*CPL* XIII ii 749). D. 11 May 1483. Also preb. of Huntington, Pratum Minus and Putson Minor. Biog. ref.: *BRUO* II 1236–7; J. Hughes, 'Martyn, Richard (d. 1483)', *ODNB* <http://www.oxforddnb.com/view/article/18236>.

M. Robert Geffrey MA ?–1494
Occ. 10 Jan. 1485 (*Reg. Myllyng* p. 95). D. 16 July 1492 × 23 Sept. 1494 (TNA, PROB 11/10; Worcestershire RO, b 716.093-BA.2648/7(ii) fo. 56v). Also chanc., treas., archdcn. of Shropshire and preb. of Inkberrow and Preston. Biog. ref.: *BRUO* II 753–4.

M. Thomas Morton BCn&CL ?–1511

Occ. 10 Apr. 1501 (TNA, PROB 11/13). D. 25 June × 20 July 1511 (TNA, PROB 11/17; *Reg. Mayew* p. 278). Also archdcn. of Shropshire and preb. of Hinton. Biog. ref.: *BRUO* II 1321–2.

M. William Webbe 1511–23

Coll. 20 July 1511 (*Reg. Mayew* p. 278). D. 2 × 29 Jan. 1523 (TNA, PROB 11/21; HCA 7031/1 fo. 32v; *Reg. Booth* p. 335). Also archdcn. of Shropshire and preb. of Gorwell and Overbury, Inkberrow, Moreton Magna and Wellington. Biog. ref.: *BRUO* III 2004.

M. John Booth SchTh 1523–42

Coll. 29 Jan. 1523 (*Reg. Booth* p. 335). Instal. 26 Sept. 1527, having previously been instal. by proxy (HCA 7031/1 fo. 40v). D. 8 × 14 Aug. 1542 (*L&P* XVII no. 581; HRO, AL 19/14 fo. 42r–v). Also preb. of Inkberrow. Biog. ref.: *BRUO 1500–40* p. 61.

ARCHDEACONS OF SHROPSHIRE

The income of the archdcn. was derived entirely from spirit. which in 1535 were valued at £32 10s 9d (*Valor* III 7).

M. Roger of Canterbury 1293–1300

Coll. 21 March 1293 (*Reg. Swinfield* p. 529). Treas. 1300. Also preb. of Hinton, Preston and Wellington.

M. Philip Talbot 1300–9

Coll. 27 Jan. 1300 (*Reg. Swinfield* p. 532). D. by 15 × 25 Apr. 1309 (*Reg. Swinfield* pp. 449–51). Also preb. of Pratum Majus.

M. John of Ross DCL ?1309–18

Occ. 29 Sept. 1308 × 28 Sept. 1309 and 15 × 25 Apr. 1309 (HCA R393; *Reg. Swinfield* pp. 449–51). Occ. 28 Oct. 1317 and res. *c.* 29 Jan. 1318 (*CPL* II 166; *Reg. Orleton* p. 60). Also preb. of Moreton Magna and Parva. Biog. ref.: *BRUO* III 1590–1; R. K. Rose, 'Ross, John (d. 1332)', *ODNB* <http://www.oxforddnb.com/view/article/24075>.

M. William son of Thomas le Mercer of Ross 1318–?

Prov. 12 June 1318 (*CPL* II 182). Papal faculty to bp. 26 Jan. 1320 to confer archdcnry. (*ibid.* 197) but William Ross occ. 2 June 1325 and 18 May 1326 (HCA 2990, 3011).

M. Richard Sydenhale 1333–?

Coll. 12 Jan 1333 (*Reg. T. Charlton* p. 78). Also treas. and preb. of Pratum Majus.

M. Henry de Shipton ?–1366

Occ. 20 Oct. 1346 (*Reg. Trillek* p. 287). Prec. 1366, probably by exch. with William Borstall. Also treas. and preb. of Hunderton and Putson Minor.

William Borstall 1366–7

Occ. 19 Sept. 1366, probably by exch. (Cant., *Reg. Langham* p. 47). Exch. 11 Dec. 1367 with Richard Nowell for ch. of Flamstead, Herts. (*Reg. L. Charlton* p. 72). Also prec. and preb. of Bartonsham. Biog. ref.: McDermid, *Beverley Fasti* pp. 72–3.

Richard Nowell 1367–?

By exch. Dec. 1367. Mistakenly called archdcn. of Hereford 12 June 1376 (*CPR 1374–7* p. 323).

John Hore ?–1410

Occ. 24 June × 28 Sept. 1385 (HCA R449). Exch. 24 July 1410 with John Wells for ch. of Eastington, Glos. (*Reg. Mascall* p. 184).

John Wells 1410

By exch. July 1410. D. by 27 Oct. (*Reg. Mascall* p. 176).

M. John Hereford or **Carpenter** BCnL 1410–17

Coll. 27 Oct. 1410 (*Reg. Mascall* p. 176). Exch. 5 May 1417 with John Loveney for archdcnry. of Hereford (*Reg. Lacy H* pp. 119, 120). Also preb. of Nonnington.

M. John Loveney 1417–22

By exch. May 1417. Exch. 21 July 1422 with John Merbury for ch. of Kedington, Suff.(?) (*Reg. Spofford* p. 368). Also archdcn. of Hereford and preb. of Withington Parva.

M. John Merbury 1422–?

By exch. July 1422. Occ. 14 Dec. 1434 (*Reg. Spofford* p. 54). Also preb. of Withington Parva.

M. William Laches or **Lathes** 1425–41

Coll. 7 Apr. 1425 (*Reg. Spofford* p. 352). D. by 28 June 1441 (*ibid.* p. 363). Also preb. of Pratum Minus. Biog. ref.: *BRUO* II 1105.

M. Thomas Yone BCnL 1441–72

Coll. 28 June 1441 (*Reg. Spofford* p. 363). Exch. 24 March 1472 with Robert Geffrey for chancellorship (*Reg. Stanbury* p. 188). Biog. ref.: *BRUO* III 2134.

M. Robert Geffrey MA 1472–?

By exch. March 1472. Occ. 16 Jan. 1478 (HCA 2923). Archdcn. of Hereford 1485. Also chanc., treas. and preb. of Inkberrow and Preston. Biog. ref.: *BRUO* II 753–4.

M. Thomas Morton BCn&CL occ. 1483, 1494

Occ. 7 Sept. 1483 and 6 Feb. 1494 (HCA 7031/1 fos. 173, 217r–v). Also archdcn. of Hereford and preb. of Hinton. Biog. ref.: *BRUO* II 1321–2.

John Martyn ?–1504

Occ. as can. and possibly archdn. 29 Sept. 1494 × 28 Sept. 1495 (HCA R531). D. as archdcn. 30 × 31 Oct. 1504 (TNA, PROB 11/14; *Reg. Mayew* p. 273). Also preb. of Bartonsham.

M. William Webbe 1504–11

Coll. 31 Oct. 1504 (*Reg. Mayew* p. 273). Archdcn. of Hereford 1511. Also preb. of Gorwell and Overbury, Inkberrow, Moreton Magna and Wellington. Biog. ref.: *BRUO* III 2004.

Arthur Stafford 1511–?

Coll. 20 July 1511 (*Reg. Mayew* p. 278).

M. John Wardroper BCn&CL ?–1515

Occ. 9 Jan. 1512 (*Reg. Mayew* p. 120). D. 16 × 27 July 1515 (TNA, PROB 11/18; *Reg. Mayew* p. 283). Also treas. and preb. of Bartonsham. Biog. ref.: *BRUO* III 1985.

M. William Goberd BA 1515

Coll. 27 July 1515 (*Reg. Mayew* p. 283). Instal. July (HCA 7031/1 fo. 6v). D. 18 Dec. 1515 (*BRUO 1500–40* p. 236). Also treas. and preb. of Moreton and Whaddon and Piona Parva. Biog. ref.: *BRUO 1500–40* p. 236.

M. Henry Martin BCn&CL 1516–24

Coll. 3 March 1516 (*Reg. Mayew* p. 284). D. 27 Jan. 1524 (*Survey of Cath.* I 555; *Reg. Booth* p. 336). Also archdcn. of Hereford and preb. of Gorwell and Overbury, Inkberrow, Norton, Warham and Withington Parva. Biog. ref.: *BRUO* II 1234.

M. Humphrey Ogle BCnL 1524–37

Coll. 28 Jan 1524 (*Reg. Booth* p. 336). Instal. 29 Jan. (HCA 7031/1 fo. 33r). Res. by 14 Aug. 1537 (*Reg. Booth* p. 378). Also preb. of Eigne and Moreton Magna. Biog. ref.: *BRUO 1500–40* p. 423.

M. Richard Sparcheford 1537–?

Expect. an archdcnry. of bp. by 10 Sept. 1535 (*L&P* IX no. 334). Coll. 14 Aug. 1537 (*Reg. Booth* p. 378). Instal. 20 Aug. (HCA 7031/1 fo. 79v). Occ. 28 June 1559 (Cant., *Reg. Parker* I 60); perhaps d. by 28 June 1560 when his preb. of Piona Parva vac. by d. of last incumbent (?Sparcheford) (HRO, AL 19/15 (Scory) fo. 1v). Biog. ref.: *BRUO 1500–40* p. 530.

PREBENDARIES OF BARTONSHAM

The endowment of this preb. was a carucate of land at Bartonsham in the parish of St Peter's, Hereford which was valued at £19 19s in 1291, 18m in 1294 and £17 18s 10d in 1535 (*Survey of Cath.* I 556; *Taxatio* p. 169b; *Reg. Swinfield* p. 305; *Valor* III 10).

Richard de Swinfield 1299–1311
   Coll. 4 Aug. 1299 (*Reg. Swinfield* p. 531). D. by 3 Aug. 1311 (*ibid.* p. 540).

M. Richard Nonnington 1311–42?
M. Robert Hereward 1320, 1324
M. Thomas Chaundos senior 1330
   Nonnington coll. 3 Aug 1311 (*Reg. Swinfield* p. 540). Resident 1316–17 to 1321–2 (HCA R407, 409–10, R125–6) and 1330–1 to 1341–2 (HCA R417, 131). Exch. 1 March 1320 with Robert Hereward for ch. of St Mawgan in Meneage, Cornwall but ineffective? (*Reg. Orleton* pp. 123, 386). Royal grs. to Hereward 16 Nov. 1320 and 12 June 1324 (*CPR 1317–24* p. 521; *CPR 1321–4* p. 423; *Reg. Orleton* p. 322). Royal gr. to Chaundos 1 June 1330 (*CPR 1327–30* p. 530) but Chaundos already archdcn. of Hereford and can. Nonnington last occ. 1 Jan. × 24 March 1342 (HCA R427). Chaundos also preb. of Eigne and unidentified preb. Biog. ref.: Hereward, *BRUO* II 915–16.

M. William Charlton BCL ?1342–80?
   First occ. as can. 24 June × 28 Sept. 1342 (HCA R427) and this preb. 18 Nov. 1366 (Cant., *Reg. Langham* p. 43). Last occ as can. 25 March × 23 June 1380 (HCA R445). Biog. ref.: *BRUO* I 393.

Roger Albrighton ?–1382
   Exch. this preb. with William Borstall 20 Feb. 1382 for preb. Funtingham in royal free chap. of Bosham, Sussex (*Reg. Gilbert* p. 123).

William Borstall 1382–9
   By exch 20 Feb. 1382. D. 13 Sept. 1389 (Lincolnshire Archives Office, Reg. XI fo. 350r). Also prec. and archdcn. of Shropshire. Biog. ref.: McDermid, *Beverley Fasti* pp. 72–3.

Reginald Braybroke 1389–92
   Royal gr. 14 Sept. 1389 (*CPR 1388–92* p. 114). Res. 30 Sept 1392 (*Reg. Trefnant* p. 192). Biog. ref.: *BRUO* I 253–4.

M. Reginald Kentwode 1392–1439
   Coll. 30 Sept. 1392 (*Reg. Trefnant* p. 177). Exch. 24 March 1439 with Geoffrey Moot for wardenship St Radegund's chap., St Paul's, London (London, GL MS. 25,513 fo. 170v, 172v). Biog. ref.: *BRUO* II 1039–40.

Geoffrey Moot 1439–?
   By exch. March 1439. D. by 28 Sept. 1453, as can.? (Exeter, *Reg. Lacy Exeter* p. 380).

M. Robert Jordan ?–1466
   Preb. of Preston from Oct. 1439. First occ. this preb. 14 June 1462 (*Reg. Stanbury* p. 75). D. 11 Feb. 1466 m.i. Hereford cath. (*Survey of Cath.* I 557).

John Persons 1466–71
   Coll. 1 Apr. 1466 (*Reg. Stanbury* p. 182). D. by 18 Sept. 1471 (*ibid.* p. 187). Also preb. of Ewithington.

M. William Chapman 1471–93/4

Coll. 18 Sept 1471 and resident until 1492–3 (*Reg. Stanbury* p. 187; HCA R508–30). D. as can. and probably this preb. 8 Oct. 1493 × 10 Feb. 1494 (TNA, PROB 11/10).

John Martyn ?1494/5–1504

First occ. as can. 29 Sept. 1494 × 28 Sept. 1495 (HCA R531). D. as preb. 30 × 31 Oct. 1504 (TNA, PROB 11/14; *Reg. Mayew* p. 273). Also archdcn. of Shropshire.

M. Robert Tehy DTh 1504–6

Coll. 31 Oct. 1504 (*Reg. Mayew* p. 273) probably until d. 7 June × 22 Nov. 1506 (TNA, PROB 11/15). Biog. ref.: *BRUO* III 1854.

John Wardroper 1506/7–15

First occ. as can. 29 Sept. 1506 × 28 Sept. 1507 (HCA R546). D. as preb. 16 × 27 July 1515 (TNA, PROB 11/18; *Reg. Mayew* p. 234). Also treas. and archdcn. of Shropshire. Biog. ref.: *BRUO* III 1985.

M. George Mason BA 1515–23

Coll. 2 Aug. 1515 (*Reg. Mayew* p. 283). Instal. by proxy 4 Aug. (HCA 7031/1 fo. 7). Exch. 27 Nov. 1523 with William Burghill for preb. of Piona Parva (*Reg. Booth* p. 336). Also preb. of Church Withington. Biog. ref.: *BRUO 1500–40* p. 386.

M. William Burghill DCnL 1523–6

By exch. Nov. 1523. Instal. 30 Nov. (HCA 7031/1 fo. 33). D. 23 Aug. 1526 (HCA 7031/1 fo. 38r). Also treas. and preb. of Piona Parva. Biog. ref.: *BRUO 1500–40* p. 85.

M. David Walker BCL 1526–47

Coll. 26 Aug. 1526 (*Reg. Booth* p. 339). Instal. 29 Aug. (HCA 7031/1 fo. 38r). D. by 1 Apr. 1547 (HRO, AL 19/14 fo. 69v). Also preb. of Moreton and Whaddon and Piona Parva. Biog. ref.: *BRUO 1500–40* p. 601.

PREBENDARIES OF BULLINGHOPE

The endowment of this preb. was two carucates of land, a mill, a dovecote and manorial dues in the manor of Bullinghope, now Bullingham, in St Martin's and All Saints parish, in Hereford which was valued at £16 1s 9d in 1291, 20m in 1294 and £16 6s 8d in 1535 (*Survey of Cath.* I 559; *Taxatio* p. 168b; V*alor* III 11).

John of Aigueblanche ?–1320

Occ. *c*.1291 (*Taxatio* p. 168; *Fasti Hereford 1066–1300* p. 32). D. 13 Feb. × 20 March 1320 (*Ch. & Rec.* pp. 186–90). Also dean.

M. Adam Murimuth DCL 1320–1

Expect. 25 Sept. 1316 (*CPL* II 123). Comm. from bp. to chapt. to carry out expect. 7 Jan. 1317 (*Reg. Swinfield* p. 520). Became preb. 1 Apr. 1320 (*Reg. Orleton* p. 130), but res. 12 Feb. 1321, as Aigueblanche's benefices were reserved to the pope (*ibid.* p. 186). Occ. as can. with unidentified preb. 1327–35. Biog. ref.: *BRUO* II 1329–30; W. R. Childs, 'Murimuth, Adam (1274/5–1347)', *ODNB* <http://www.oxforddnb.com/view/article/19567>.

M. John Walwayn DCL 1322
M. Stephen of Ledbury DCL 1323–53

Coll. to Walwyn 1 Feb. 1322 (*Reg. Orleton* p. 220). Prov. to Ledbury, on strength of above reservn., 16 Sept. 1323 (*CPL* II 234), and he d. as preb. by 17 Apr. 1353 (*Reg. Trillek* p. 387). Ledbury also dean; Walwayn also preb. of Wellington. Biog. ref.: Walwayn, *BRUO* III 2225; Ledbury, *BRUO* II 1121.

M. William Wroth DCL 1353–66?
William de Dalton 1354

Coll. to Wroth 17 Apr. 1353 (*Reg. Trillek* p. 387). Expect. 2 July 1343 and occ. as can. 25 March × 23 June 1353 (*CPL* III 132; *CPP* p. 60; HCA R432). Prov. to Dalton 24 Jan. 1354 (*L&G* p. 98; *CPP* p. 279). Papal conf. of Wroth as preb. 13 Oct. 1355 (*CPL* II 279, 289). Wroth occ. 24 Aug. 1366 (HCA 1475). Biog. ref.: *BRUO* III 2095.

M. Philip Ace ?1366–?
M. Griffin Charlton BCL 1366/7
M. John of Bedwardine or Smythes 1367–70
Thomas Arundel 1369–73
John Sleford 1369–70

Prov. to Ace 15 Dec. 1362 (*CPP* pp. 387–8). Coll. to Charlton 1366–7, although Charlton was already preb. Piona Parva and remained so (Cant., *Reg. Langham* p. 40; *CPR 1370–4* pp. 19–20). While suit at curia was pending Charlton arranged for a royal gr. 4 Dec. 1367 to Bedwardine (*ibid* p. 42), while he continued to enjoy the revenues. Royal lic. to Ace 28 Jan. 1368 to plead in person at the curia (*ibid* p. 127). Ace d. at curia by 2 Aug. 1369 and the pope surrogated Arundel into his rights (*L&G* p. 360). Prov. Ace's preb. to Arundel 2 Aug. 1369 (*ibid.*).

Writ of *Quare impedit* served on Charlton for keeping the revenues, and Bedwardine instal., but he res. secretly, *sede vacante*, and arranged for a royal gr. 15 July 1369 to Sleford (*CPR 1367–70* p. 278), while he continued to enjoy the revenues. On 23 Nov. 1370 k. revoked all grs. concerning the preb. and gave Arundel permission to plead at the curia (*CPR 1370–4* p. 19). Arundel gained possession by 17 March 1372 (*Original Papal Letters in England 1305–1415*, ed. P. N. R. Zutshi (Index Actorum Romanorum Pontificum, v, Vatican City, 1990) no. 324). Bp. Ely 1373. Biog. ref.: Charlton, *BRUO* I 390; Arundel, *BRUO* I 51–3; J. Hughes, 'Arundel, Thomas (1353–1414)', *ODNB* <http://www.oxforddnb.com/view/article/713>.

M. John of Bedwardine or **Smythes** (again) occ. 1374
M. Nicholas Drayton LicCL 1377–9

Bedwardine's estate ratif. 30 Aug. 1374 (*CPR 1374–7* p. 1). Prov. to Drayton 17 Feb. 1371 who claimed this preb. after he had proved in the royal cts. that Bedwardine could have no right by the k. to it, and was gr. permission to plead at curia, 20 Feb. 1377 (*Lettres Gregoire XI* no. 13932; *CPR 1374–7* p. 432). Drayton d. by 9 March 1379 and Bedwardine res. the archdcnry. of Hereford and perhaps this preb. 2 Apr. 1379 (*CPP* p. 547; *Reg. Gilbert* p. 6). Biog. ref.: Drayton, *BRUC* p. 194; A. B. Cobban, 'Drayton, Nicholas (d. in or before 1379)', *ODNB* <http://www.oxforddnb.com/view/article/8043>.

Richard Roter 1379
John Waltham junior ?1379–83

Prov. by anti-pope Clement VIII to Roter 9 March 1379 (*CPP* p. 547). Waltham occ. as can. 10 April × 23 June 1379 (HCA R444a) and this preb. 28 Apr. 1380 (*CPR 1377–80* p. 463). Exch. 8 May 1383 with Nicholas Hethe for preb. of South Cave in York (York, Borthwick Institute, Reg. 12 fo. 34). Biog. ref.: Waltham, R. G. Davies, 'Waltham, John (d. 1395)', *ODNB* <http://www.oxforddnb.com/view/article/28645>.

M. Nicholas Hethe 1383–90

By exch. May 1383. It was decided that the preb. would be annexed to the deanery when vac. by Hethe (*Reg Gilbert* pp. 97–8; *CPR 1381–5* p. 525). Hethe d. by 24 Aug. 1390 (*Reg. Trefnant* p. 174). Also preb. of Hunderton. Biog. ref.: *BRUC* p. 302.

M. John Harold BCn&CL 1390–3

Harold's right as dean to the preb. conf. by k. 27 June 1389 (*Reg. Trefnant* p. 73). Coll. 24 Aug. 1390 (*ibid.* pp. 64, 174). Chapt. in dispute with bp. over this and later Trefnant claimed the coll. was an act of grace and refused to recognize the annexation to the deanery (*ibid.* pp. 58–100). D. 19 Oct. 1393 (*ibid.* p. 56). Also preb. of Moreton and Whaddon and Norton. Biog. ref.: *BRUO* II 877.

Richard Kingston 1393–?

Coll. 19 Oct. 1393 (*Reg. Trefnant* p. 177). Chapt. refused to induct on grounds that preb. was annexed to deanery (*ibid.* pp. 58–9). Appeal to Canterbury Feb. 1394, to Rome 1395 (*ibid.* pp. 62–73). On 26 May 1396 bp. offered to create new preb. out of his own lands to be united to deanery, but chapt. declined offer, 3 June (*ibid.* pp. 92–5). Union annulled 3 Apr. 1397 by Boniface IX (*ibid.* p. 98). Kingston occ. 27 Oct. 1397 (*CPL* V 73). Preb. Norton 1418 but ineffective. May have res. preb. when res. archdcnry. of Hereford in Jan. 1405. Also claimed preb. of Cublington. Biog. ref.: McDermid, *Beverley Fasti* pp. 64–5.

William Lochard ?1416/17–38/9

First occ. as can. 29 Sept. 1416 × 28 Sept. 1417 (HCA R470), as this preb. 2 Dec. 1429 (*CPL* VIII 158). D. as can. 11 Apr. 1438 × 29 Apr. 1439 (TNA, PROB 11/3). Also prec.

William Middleham ?1439–63

Preb. of Eigne from 1432. Resident until d. Probably this preb. after d. of Lochard. Occ. this preb. 14 June 1463 (*Reg. Stanbury* pp. 74–5). D. by 4 Dec. 1463 (*ibid.* p. 179). Also prec. and treas.

M. John Grene or **Holder** BCL 1463–72

Coll. 4 Dec. 1463 (*Reg. Stanbury* p. 179). D. by 31 March 1472 (*ibid.* p. 188). Also preb. of Gorwell and Overbury and Hampton. Biog. ref.: *BRUO* II 819.

M. Richard Rudhale DCnL 1472–6

Coll. 31 March 1472 (*Reg. Stanbury* p. 188). D. 16 May × 20 July 1476 (TNA, PROB 11/6). Also treas., archdcn. of Hereford and preb. of Huntington. Biog. ref.: *BRUO* III 1603.

M. Richard Judde BCnL ?1488/9–1512

Occ. as can. 29 Sept. 1488 × 28 Sept. 1489 (HCA R526) and continuously resident until d. D. this preb. 12 May 1512 (*Reg. Mayew* p. 182). Also treas.

M. Richard Smythe DCnL 1512–16

Coll. 26 May 1512 (*Reg. Mayew* p. 279). Res. by 7 July 1516 (*L&P* II i no. 2140). Also preb. of Inkberrow. Biog. ref.: *BRUO* III 1718.

William Bolton O.Can.S.A., prior of St Bartholomew's Smithfield 1516–32

Royal gr. 7 July 1516 (*L&P* II i no. 2140). Instal. by 17 Nov. (HCA 7031/1 fo. 8v). Abp.'s man. adm. 22 Nov. 1516; second instal. 28 Nov. (*ibid.* fo. 9r). Gr. lic. to treat with Welshe for pension 29 Aug. 1531 (*Reg. Booth* p. 346). D. by 8 Apr. 1532 (*Reg. Booth* p. 346). Biog. ref.: *BRUO 1500–40* p. 56; J. Etherton, 'Bolton, William (d. 1532)', *ODNB* <http://www.oxforddnb.com/view/article/2809>.

Edward Welshe 1532–54

Coll. 8 Apr. 1532 (*Reg. Booth* p. 346). Instal. 10 Apr. (HCA 7031/1 fo. 69v). Depriv. 2 Apr. 1554 by dean and chapt. *sede vacante* as a married priest (HCA 7031/1 fo. 125r–v).

PREBENDARIES OF CHURCH WITHINGTON

The endowment of this preb. was land, rents and labour services in the manor of Withington, Herefs., close to the parish ch. which were valued at £7 1s 4d in 1291, 15m in 1294 and £15 in 1535 (*Survey of Cath.* I 565; *Taxatio* p. 169b; *Reg. Swinfield* p. 305; *Valor* III 10).

Peter of Savoy 1290–1308

Coll. 23 Dec. 1290 (*Reg. Swinfield* pp. 135–6, 152–3, 528). Abp. of Lyons prov. 7 Aug. 1308 (*Reg. Clement V* no. 2895).

Hugh of Leominster 1310?, 1317–27
M. Thomas Charlton DCL 1317

Royal request to bp. for preb. for Leominster 30 Dec. 1308 (*Reg. Swinfield* p. 444). Leominster first occ. as can. 25 March × 23 June 1310 (HCA R394), this preb? Royal gr. to Charlton 7 Apr. 1317 (*CPR 1313–17* p. 636). Royal gr. to Leominster 6 June 1317 (*CPR 1313–17* p. 659). His proxy instal., but chapt. refused to install Leominster in person. Royal mand. adm. to bp., 10 Dec. (*CPR 1317–21* p. 64; *Reg. Orleton* p. 51). Leominster last occ. as can. 29 Sept. 1327 × 28 Sept. 1328 (HCA R127). Charlton also bp. of Hereford. Biog. ref.: Charlton, *BRUO* I 392; D. Lepine, 'Charlton, Thomas (*c*.1292–1344)', *ODNB* <http://www.oxforddnb.com/view/article/5168>.

Roger Mortimer 1327–32

Royal gr. 13 Dec. 1327; prohibns. in his favour, 20 Jan. 1328 (*CPR 1327–30* pp. 196, 203). Occ. 29 Sept. × 31 Dec. 1327 (HCA R414). D. by 26 Apr. 1332 (*CCR 1330–3* p. 560).

Simon de Northwood 1332–?

Expect. 13 June 1329 (*CPL* II 292). Proctor instal., but could not obtain possession of prebendal manor. Royal writ 26 Apr. 1332 for expulsion of occupiers (*CCR 1330–3* p. 560). Occ. 24 Sept. 1335 (*CPL* II 531).

M. Robert de Chickwell ?1337–9

Occ. as can. 25 March × 23 June 1337 (HCA R422); estate ratif. this preb. 18 Apr. 1337 (*CPR 1334–8* pp. 419, 425). Exch. 21 May 1339 with Michael Northburgh for preb. Lyme and Halstock in Salisbury (J. Le Neve, *Fasti Ecclesiae Anglicanae 1300–1541*, iii: *Salisbury*, comp. J. M. Horn (1962) p. 64). Biog. ref.: *Hemingby's Register* pp. 190–1.

M. Michael Northburgh DCL 1339–54

By exch. May 1339. Bp. of London 1354. Biog. ref.: *BRUO* II 1368–70; R. M. Haines, 'Northburgh, Michael (*c*.1300–61)', *ODNB* <http://www.oxforddnb.com/view/article/20324>.

M. William Somerford DCL 1354–61

Reservn. Northburgh's preb. 15 Dec. 1354 (*CPL* III 530); first occ. as can. 25 March × 23 June 1355 (HCA R434). D. by 12 July 1361 (*CPR 1361–4* p. 42). Biog. ref.: *BRUO* II 2217.

William of Wykeham 1361–2

Royal gr. 12 July 1361 (*CPR 1361–4* p. 42; HCA 2780). Exch. 15 Feb. 1362 with William Burghbridge for preb. of Crowhurst in royal free chap. of Hastings (*CPR 1361–4* pp. 167–8). Biog. ref.: P. Partner, 'Wykeham, William (*c*.1324–1404)', *ODNB* <http://www.oxforddnb.com/view/article/30127>.

M. William Burghbridge 1362–91

By exch. Feb. 1362. Bp.'s mand. adm. 12 March (HCA 2781). Exch. 15 Apr. 1391 with John Chitterne for preb. of Swallowcliffe in Heytesbury, Wilts. (*Reg. Trefnant* p. 188).

M. John Chitterne 1391–1419
M. William Corfe DTh 1413
Chitterne became preb. by exch. Apr. 1391. Coll. to Corfe 3 Oct. 1413, on alleged d. of Chitterne (*Reg. Mascall* p. 178). But Chitterne d. as preb. 20 × 28 Apr. 1419 (TNA, PROB 11/2B; *Reg. Lacy H* p. 115). Biog. ref.: Chitterne, Richardson, *Chancery* pp. 91–2; Corfe, *BRUO* I 487.

M. John Cokworthy 1419–22
Coll. 28 Apr. 1419 (*Reg. Lacy H* p. 115). Exch. 13 Nov. 1422 with Thomas Guldefeld for vic. of Sutton by Plymouth, Devon (*Reg. Spofford* p. 368; Exeter, *Reg. Lacy Exeter* p. 58). Also preb. of Warham.

Thomas Guldefeld 1422–7
By exch. Nov. 1422. D. by 23 Sept. 1427 (*Reg. Spofford* p. 354). Also preb. of Cublington.

M. Nicholas Mallon 1427–41
Coll. 23 Sept. 1427 (*Reg. Spofford* p. 354). Exch. 12 March 1441 with William Hambald for ch. of Patrick Brompton, Yorks. (*ibid.* p. 369).

William Hambald 1441–?
By exch. March 1441. Occ. 19 Sept. 1446 (Exeter, *The Register of Edmund Lacy, Bishop of Exeter 1420–55: Registrum Commune*, ed. G. Dunstan (5 vols., Canterbury and York Soc., lx–lxiii, lxvi, 1963–72) III 287). D. 23 Nov. 1453 × 2 May 1455, as preb? (TNA, PROB 11/4).

M. William Dorset DCL occ. 1462
Occ. 6 June 1462 (*Reg. Stanbury* p. 76). D. by 14 Feb. 1471, as preb? (J. Silvester Davies, *A History of Southampton* (Southampton, 1883) p. 348). Biog. ref.: *BRUO* I 544–5.

M. James Bromwich BCnL ?1494/5–1524
First occ. as can. 29 Sept. 1494 × 28 Sept. 1495 (HCA R531). Occ. this preb. 23 June 1512 (*CPL* XIX no. 820). D. 3 Feb. × 16 Apr. 1524 (HCA 7031/1 fo. 34; *Reg. Booth* p. 337). Also chanc. Biog. ref.: *BRUO* I 277.

M. George Mason BA 1524–39
Coll. 16 Apr. 1524 (*Reg. Booth* p. 337). Instal. 27 Sept. (HCA 7031/1 fo. 36r). Res. by 4 Aug. 1539 (*Reg. Booth* p. 385). Also preb. of Bartonsham and Piona Parva. Biog. ref.: *BRUO 1500–40* p. 386.

William Lewson or **Leveson** BCL 1539–83
Coll. 4 Aug. 1539 (*Reg. Booth* p. 385). Instal. s.d. (HCA 7031/1 fo. 84r). In 1561 thought to be harbouring John Blaxton and Walter Mugg, recusant prebs. of Exeter, in Herefs. (Calendar of State Papers Domestic, Addenda 1547–65 p. 522) and still late 1564 ('A collection of original letters from the bishops to the privy council, 1564', ed. M. Bateson, *Camden Miscellany IX* (Camden Soc., new ser., liii, 1893)

p. 19). D. 23 Feb. × 9 Apr. 1583 (HCA 7031/2 fo. 105r; Devon RO, Chanter 21 fo. 8r); chancellorship of Exeter vac., probably by his d., by 23 March (Devon RO, Chanter 41 p. 307).

PREBENDARIES OF COLWALL (BARTON IN COLWALL)

The endowment of this preb. was two carucates of land and rent in Barton in the parish of Colwall, Herefs., which was valued at £13 6s 8d in 1291, 15m in 1294 and £15 4s 4d in 1535 (*Survey of Cath.* I 561; *Taxatio* p. 169b; *Reg. Swinfield* p. 305; V*alor* III 8).

M. William de Sardene DCL 1297–1303
Coll. 17 June 1297 (*Reg. Swinfield* p. 530). D. as preb. 5 Nov. 1303 (*ibid.* pp. 395, 535). Biog. ref.: *BRUO* III 1641–2.

John of Kempsey 1303–17
Coll. 8 Nov. 1303 (*Reg. Swinfield* p. 535). D. 9 × 26 May 1317 (HCA 1028, 2880). Also treas. and preb. of Moreton Parva.

Thomas of Pembridge 1317–29
Royal gr. 18 May 1317 (*CPR 1313–17* p. 651). D. by 24 Oct. 1329 (*Reg. T. Charlton* p. 76). Also treas.

M. John Ewe or **Oo of Oxford** 1329–54
John de Gerdone or **Geydon** 1329
Coll. to Ewe 24 Oct. 1329 (*Reg. T. Charlton* p. 76). Gerdone had expect. 25 June 1325 (*CPL* II 246), adm. by bp. 31 Oct. 1329 and occ. as can. 29 Sept. × 31 Dec. 1329 (*Reg. T. Charlton* p. 76; HCA R416). But Ewe continued to hold it and d. as preb. by 10 Dec. 1354 (*Reg. Trillek* p. 387). Ewe also prec. and treas. Biog. ref.: Ewe, *BRUO* II 1399.

Thomas Rous 1355–69?
Expect. 20 Apr. 1353 (*CPL* III 478). First occ. as can. 25 March × 23 June 1355 and occ. this preb. 4 Aug. 1366 (HCA R434; Cant., *Reg. Langham*, p. 5). Held canonical house 10 Feb. 1367 to 26 March 1369 (*Reg. L. Charlton* pp. 67, 69).

M. John Cateby LicCL ?1384–90
First occ. as can. 25 March × 23 June 1384 (HCA R448). Estate ratif. this preb. 1 June 1390 (*CPR 1388–92* p. 256). Res. it by 25 Sept. (*Reg. Trefnant* p. 175).

M. John Barnet junior LicCL 1390–?
Coll 25 Sept. 1390 (*Reg. Trefnant* p. 175). Biog. ref.: *BRUO* I 113–14.

M. John Cateby DCnL (again) ?1393–1411
Occ. 7 Nov. 1393 as can. and regularly to 24 June × 28 Sept. 1409 (*Reg. Trefnant* p. 57; HCA R457–64). D. as preb. by 11 Feb. 1411 (*Reg. Mascall* p. 176).

John Sutton 1411–16

Coll. 11 Feb. 1411 (*Reg. Mascall* p. 176). D. by 12 June 1416 (*ibid.* p. 181).

M. John Bridbroke LicCL 1416–27

Coll. 12 June 1416 (*Reg. Mascall* p. 181). Exch. 23 July 1427 with Henry Shelford for ch. of Sudbourne, Suff. (*Reg. Spofford* p. 369). Also prec. Biog. ref.: *BRUC* pp. 92–3.

Henry Shelford 1427–45/6

By exch. July 1427. Last occ. as can. 29 Sept. 1445 × 28 Sept. 1446 (HCA R484). Also dean. Biog. ref.: Richardson, *Chancery* pp. 80–1.

M. John Arundel DM 1456/7–9

First occ. as can. 29 Sept. 1456 × 28 Sept. 1457 (HCA R494). Res. this preb. by 19 Jan. 1459 to become bp. of Chichester (*Reg. Stanbury* p. 176). Biog. ref.: *BRUO* I 49–50; C. Whittick, 'Arundel, John (*c.*1400–77)', *ODNB* <http://www.oxforddnb.com/view/article/719>.

M. Thomas Manning DCnL 1459–62

Coll. 19 Apr. 1459 (*Reg. Stanbury* p. 176). Attainted 1461 and res. by 13 Apr. 1462 (*ibid.* p. 178). Also preb. of Gorwell and Overbury. Biog. ref.: *BRUO* II 1216–17.

Robert Stanbury 1462–4

Coll. 13 Apr. 1462 (*Reg. Stanbury* p. 176). D. by 8 June 1464 (*ibid.* p. 180).

Edmund Audley 1464–80

Coll. 8 June 1464 (*Reg. Stanbury* p. 178). Bp. of Rochester 1480 and Hereford 1492. Biog. ref.: *BRUO* II 75–6; J. Hughes, 'Audley, Edmund (*c.*1439–1524)', *ODNB* <http://www.oxforddnb.com/view/article/891>.

M. David Hopton BCnL 1480–92

Coll. 18 Sept. 1480 (*Reg. Myllyng* p. 191). D. 16 Jan. 1491 × 29 Jan. 1492 (TNA, PROB 11/9; Salisbury, *The Register of Thomas Langton, Bishop of Salisbury 1485–1493*, ed. D. P. Wright (Canterbury and York Soc., lxxiv, 1985) no. 333). Also preb. of Nonnington.

M. Richard Bromefeld BCnL 1492–1518

Coll. 19 Feb. 1492 (Canterbury, *The Register of John Morton, Archbishop of Canterbury 1486–1500*, ed. C. Harper-Bill (3 vols., Canterbury and York Soc., lxxv, lxxviii, lxxxix, 1987–2000) I no. 519). D. 24 Oct. 1518 (*Reg. Booth* p. 332). Biog. ref.: *BRUC* p. 96.

M. Edmund Frouceter DTh 1518–29

Coll. 28 Oct. 1518 (*Reg. Booth* p. 332). D. 16 May 1529 (*ibid.* p. 213). Also dean, treas. and preb. of Norton and Putson Major. Biog. ref.: *BRUO* II 732.

M. Gamaliel Clifton DCnL 1529–41

Coll. 16 May 1529 (*Reg. Booth* p. 342). Instal. by proxy 17 May (HCA 7031/1 fo. 46v). D. 29 Apr. 1541 (HRO, AL 19/14 fo. 24r). Also dean and preb. of Pratum Minus. Biog. ref.: *BRUC* p. 141.

M. William Wilbram BA 1541–61

Coll. 24 Aug. 1541 (HRO, AL 19/14 fo. 31r–v). Instal. 13 Sept. (HCA 7031/1 fo 86r). Accounted for first fruits 14 Sept. (TNA, E 334/2 fo. 55r). On pardon roll 15 Jan. 1559 (*CPR 1558–60* p. 231). D. as preb. 8 Sept. 1561 (HCA 7031/1 fo. 206v). Biog. ref.: *BRUO 1500–40* p. 628.

PREBENDARIES OF CUBLINGTON (MADLEY)

The endowment of this preb. was a carucate of land, rents, labour services, an acre of meadow, a garden, dovecote and revenue in milk and cheese in Cublington in the parish of Madley, Herefs., which was valued at £6 9s in 1291, 18m in 1294 and £12 6s 8d in 1535 (*Survey of Cath.* I 563; *Taxatio* p. 169a; *Reg. Swinfield* p. 305; *Valor* III 11).

M. Roger of Sevenoaks 1280–1300

First occ. as can. 1277 × 1282 and 4 March 1278 (HCA 1412; *Reg. Cantilupe* p. 171). Coll. to this preb. 17 Apr. 1280 (*ibid.* p. 63). D. by 15 Jan. 1300 (*Reg. Swinfield* p. 531). Also treas.

William de Mortimer 1300–16

Coll. 15 Jan. 1300 (*Reg. Swinfield* p. 531). D. by 15 Sept. 1316 (*ibid.* p. 544). Also preb. of Gorwell and Overbury.

John de la Felde 1316–38?

Coll. 15 Sept. 1316 (*Reg. Swinfield* p. 544). Last occ. 25 March × 23 June 1338 (HCA R423), counted as resident pro rata 1338–9 (HCA R130).

M. William of Sheynton BCL ?1338–66

Probably can. as well as archdcn. Hereford, occ. continuously in accounts from 24 June × 28 Sept. 1338 until 24 June × 28 Sept. 1361 (HCA R425–38). Occ. this preb. 18 Nov. 1366 (Cant., *Reg. Langham* p. 43). D. 20 Dec. 1366 (*Calendar of Inquisitions Post Mortem* XII no. 168).

M. William Durant BTh ?1371–5

Reservn. preb. and dig. 24 Nov. 1362, repeated 24 Dec. 1363 (*Lettres Urbain V* nos. 4630, 11251). Occ. this preb. 28 Jan. 1371 (*Lettres Gregoire XI* no. 9613) and as can. 29 Sept. × 31 Dec. 1372 (HCA R440). D. as can. 29 Sept. × 31 Dec. 1375 (HCA R442; *BRUO* I 612). Biog. ref.: *BRUO* I 612.

M. Thomas de Chaundos junior 1375

Expect. and reservn. preb. 25 Feb. 1371 (*L&G* p. 420; *Lettres Gregoire XI* no. 13965). Occ. 20 Oct. 1375 (*CPR 1374–7* p. 177). Preb. Putson Minor 1376.

M. John de Middleton DTh ?1376–94
Richard Kingston 1391

Middleton had an expect. of preb. and dig. 28 Jan. 1371 (*L&G* p. 430). Occ. as can. continuously from 25 March × 23 June 1376 until 25 March × 24 June 1394 and occ. this preb. *c*.1375–6 (HCA R443–56; *L&G* p. 497). Estate ratif. 28 March 1388 (*CPR 1385–8* p. 430). Royal gr. to Kingston 5 June 1391 (*CPR 1388–92* p. 412) but ineffective. Kingston became preb. of Bullinghope 1393 and Middleton d. as preb of Cublington by 27 June 1394 (*Reg. Trefnant* p. 178). Kingston also archdcn. of Hereford and preb. of Norton; Middleton also dean. Biog. ref.: Middleton, *BRUO* II 1276; Kingston, McDermid, *Beverley Fasti* pp. 64–5.

Thomas Guldefeld 1394–1402?

Coll. 27 June 1394 (*Reg. Trefnant* pp. 178; *CPR 1391–6* p. 467). Last occ. as can. 24 June × 28 Sept. 1402 (HCA R462). Also preb. of Church Withington.

Thomas Bushbury 1403–9

Coll. 28 Feb. 1403 (*Reg. Trefnant* p. 186). D. 29 March 1409 m.i., Ashbury, Berks. (*Survey of Cath.* I 563). Also preb. of Moreton Parva.

M. John Pavy BCL 1409–14

Coll. 31 March 1409 (*Reg. Mascall* p. 174). D. 18 × 22 May 1414 (Cant., *Reg. Chichele* II 1–2). Biog. ref.: *BRUO* III 1438–9.

M. John Stanway BCL 1414–34

Coll. 22 May 1414 (*Reg. Mascall* p. 179). D. 9 Aug. 1434 (*Reg. Spofford* p. 179). Also dean.

M. John Asheby 1434–64

Coll. 9 Aug. 1434 (*Reg. Spofford* p. 179). D. by 16 Aug. 1464 (*Reg. Stanbury* p. 180). Also chanc., treas. and preb. of Moreton Parva.

M. Simon Tawre BCnL 1464–76

Coll. 16 Aug. 1464 (*Reg. Stanbury* p. 180). Res. by 27 Sept. 1476; d. by 8 Oct. (*Reg. Myllyng* pp. 186–7). Also chanc. and preb. of Warham. Biog. ref.: *BRUO* III 1850.

M. John Arundel BTh 1476–96

Coll. 27 Sept. 1476 (*Reg. Myllyng* p. 186). Bp. of Coventry and Lichfield 1496. Also chanc. and treas. Biog. ref.: *BRUO* I 50–1; N. I. Orme, 'Arundel, John (*c*.1435–1503)', *ODNB* <http://www.oxforddnb.com/view/article/720>.

M. Peter Carmelian ?–1527

Occ. in Mayew's episcopate 1504 × 16 (*Reg. Mayew* p. 234). Vac. by 4 June 1527 (HCA 7031/1 fo. 39v). Biog. ref.: *BRUO* I 358–9; J. B. Trapp, 'Carmelian, Peter (*c*.1451–1527)', *ODNB* <http://www.oxforddnb.com/view/article/4699>.

M. Peter Vannes BTh 1527–63

Instal. by proxy 4 June 1527 and again in person 7 Aug. 1532 (HCA 7031/1 fos. 39v, 70r). Occ. 2 Jan. 1561 (HCA 7031/1 fo. 201v). D. 28 March × 1 May 1563 (Salisbury Cath. Library, Chapter Acts 15 fo. 2v/p. 2; TNA, PROB 11/46). Biog. ref.: McDermid, *Beverley Fasti* p. 67.

PREBENDARIES OF EIGNE

The endowment of this preb. was rents in Eigne and Aylestone and half an acre of meadow in the parish of Hampton Bishop, Herefs., which was valued at £2 18s 6d in 1291, 10s in 1294 and £3 9s 5d in 1535 (*Survey of Cath.* I 606; *Taxatio* p. 169a; *Reg. Swinfield* p. 305; *Valor* III 12).

M. Thomas of St Omer ?1273/4–1305/6?

First occ. as can. 1 Nov. 1273 × 24 March 1274 (HCA R2a). Occ. this preb. 1291 and 23 March 1297 (*Taxatio* p. 169a; *CPR 1292–1301* p. 278). Last occ. 29 Sept. 1305 × 28 Sept. 1306 (HCA R390).

M. Thomas Chaundos senior 1317–?

Royal gr. 31 May 1317 and occ. as can. 24 June × 28 Sept. (*CPR 1313–17* p. 655; HCA R407). Archdcn. Hereford 1319 until 1332 and also can. with unidentified preb. and preb. of Bartonsham.

John de Oxyndon 1320–37

Coll. 19 Oct. 1320 (*Reg. Orleton* p. 386). Estate ratif. 22 Feb. 1335 (*CPR 1334–8* p. 80). D. by 12 March 1337 (*CCR 1337–9* pp. 107–8). Biog. ref.: *Hemingby's Register*, p. 218.

Robert Henley ?1337–66?

First occ. as can. 1 Jan. × 24 March 1337 and almost continuously resident until 24 June × 28 Sept. 1361 (HCA R422–38). Occ. this preb. 18 Nov. 1366 (Cant., *Reg. Langham* p. 42).

M. Roger Sutton DCL ?–1368

Expect. 22 Feb. 1363, not yet effected by 26 March 1366 (*CPP* pp. 404, 519). Exch. this preb. 29 Oct. 1368 with William Birmingham for preb. of Moreton and Whaddon (*Reg. L. Charlton* p. 72). Also archdcn. of Hereford. Biog. ref.: *BRUC* p. 568.

M. William Birmingham DTh 1368–82

By exch. Oct. 1368. D. by 30 Apr. 1382 (Exeter, *Reg. Brantingham* p. 77). Also dean and preb. of Moreton and Whaddon. Biog. ref.: *BRUO* I 177.

John Ganvill ?–1401

Estate ratif. 1 Dec. 1391 (*CPR 1388–92* p. 512) and 8 Nov. 1399 (*CPR 1399–1401* p. 54). Exch. with Gilbert Stone for preb. of Wedmore II in Wells, deanery of Hastings and preb. Wilmcote in Tamworth, Staffs.; royal gr. to Ganvill of Stone's benefices 5 March 1401 (*ibid.* pp. 442–3).

M. Gilbert Stone 1401–14

By exch. Coll. 23 March 1401 (*Reg. Trefnant* p. 186; Chichester, *The Episcopal Register of Robert Reade, Ordinis Predicatorum, Lord Bishop of Chichester 1397–1415*, ed. C. Deedes (Sussex Record Soc., viii, xi, 1908–10) I 260–1). Exch. 12 Oct. 1414 with John Clere for ch. of Imber, Wilts. (*Reg. Mascall* p. 187). Biog. ref.: *BRUO* III 1787–8.

John Clere 1414–18

By exch. 12 Oct. 1414. Res. by 1 Feb. 1418 (*Reg. Lacy H* p. 118).

Edmund le Bord 1418–19

Comm. to coll. 6 Feb. 1418 (*Reg. Lacy H* pp. 114, 118). Occ. as preb. 29 Sept. 1418 × 28 Sept. 1419 (HCA R636). D. by 19 Dec. 1419 (*ibid.* p. 116).

Hugh Buyton 1419–30

Coll. 19 Dec. 1419 (*Reg. Lacy H* p. 116). Exch. by 23 Aug. 1430 with John Mapleton for ch. of Eccleston, Ches. (HCA 2790).

John Mapleton 1430–2

By exch. Aug. 1430. D. by 23 Oct. 1432 (*Reg. Spofford* p. 358). Biog. ref.: Richardson, *Chancery* pp. 78–9.

William Middleham 1432–9?

Coll. 23 Oct. 1432 (*Reg. Spofford* p. 358). Occ. as preb. 5 Sept. 1434 (HCA 2900). A can. until d. by 4 Dec 1463 (*Reg. Stanbury* p. 179); preb. Bullinghope occ. June 1463, probably from d. of previous incumbent in 1439. Also prec. and treas.

M. John Paslewe BCn&CL ?–1447

Res. this preb. 5 June 1447 (*Reg. Spofford* p. 367).

M. Ralph Durward 1447–62?

Coll. 5 June 1447 (*Reg. Spofford* p. 367). D. by 3 Aug. 1462, probably by 14 June, as can.? (London, GL MS. 9531/7 fo. 82v; *Reg. Stanbury* p. 76; *BRUC* p. 202). Biog. ref.: *BRUC* p. 202.

M. Richard Hewes 1462

Occ. 14 June 1462 (*Reg. Stanbury* p. 76).

M. Nicholas Rawdon ?1463/4–?

Occ. this preb. 29 Sept. 1463 × 28 Sept. 1464 and 29 Sept. 1467 × 28 Sept. 1468 (HCA R637a, 637c).

M. Oliver King DCL ?–1481

Res. this preb. by 13 Jan. 1481 (*Reg. Myllyng* p. 191). Also dean. Biog. ref.: *BRUC* pp. 343–4; S. J. Gunn, 'King, Oliver (d. 1503)', *ODNB* <http://www.oxforddnb.com/view/article/15580>.

M. William Skyby MA 1481–8

Coll. 13 Jan. 1481 (*Reg. Myllyng* p. 191). D. by 12 June 1488 (*ibid.* p. 196).

M. Ralph Hauyes BCnL 1488–9

Coll. 12 June 1488 (*Reg. Myllyng* p. 196). Preb. Wellington after March 1489 (*ibid.* p. 197). Also preb. of Piona Parva.

M. Nicholas Walwen ?1501/2–1512

First occ. as can. 29 Sept. 1501 × 28 Sept. 1502 (HCA R541) and this preb. in Mayew's episcopate (1504 × 16) (*Reg. Mayew* p. 234). Occ. as holding this preb. 13 Sept. 1513 (HCA 7031/1 fo. 1), but res. by 26 Oct. 1512 to become preb. of Moreton Parva (*ibid.* p. 280). Also treas. Biog. ref.: *BRUO 1500–40* p. 707.

M. William Delabere 1512–21

Coll. 26 Oct. 1512 (*Reg. Mayew* p. 280). D. by 1 March 1521 (*Reg. Booth* p. 333). Also preb. of Piona Parva and Pratum Majus.

M. Humphrey Ogle BCnL 1521–3

Coll. 1 March 1521 (*Reg. Booth* p. 333). Preb. of Moreton Magna 1523 (*Reg. Booth* p. 335). Also archdcn. of Shropshire. Biog. ref.: *BRUO 1500–40* p. 423.

M. Roger Benlloyde 1523–33

Coll. 30 Jan. 1523 (*Reg. Booth* p. 333). Instal. 12 March (HCA 7031/1 fo. 32v). D. by 1 Feb. 1533 (*Reg. Booth* p. 347). Biog. ref.: *BRUO 1500–40* p. 663.

M. William Chell BMus 1533–45

Coll. 1 Feb. 1533 (*Reg. Booth* p. 347). Instal. 28 Feb. (HCA 7031/1 fo. 70v). Preb. of Ewithington 1545. Biog. ref.: *BRUO 1500–40* p. 115; R. Woodley, 'Chelle, William (*fl.* 1524–59)', *ODNB* <http://www.oxforddnb.com/view/article/5212>.

PREBENDARIES OF THE PREBENDA EPISCOPI

This preb. acts as penitentiary

The preb., known variously as Prebenda Episcopi, the Bishop's Prebend, the Golden Prebend and Prebend Poenitentiarii, was founded by bp. Ralph of Maidstone (1234–9) to provide for the penitentiary. There was no endowment and it is not listed in the 1291 *Taxatio*. The 1294 valuation states that the penitentiary received only the commons other cans. were entitled to (*Reg. Swinfield* p. 305). In 1535 the preb. was valued at £1 17s 8d, the value of small commons that year (*Valor* III 9). The penitentiary was required to reside continuously (*Ch. & Rec.* p. 228).

Hugh de Braose 1293–1320

Coll. 9 July 1293 (*Reg. Swinfield* p. 529). D. by 21 Dec. 1320 (HCA 823; *Reg. Orleton* p. 386).

William de Wyke 1320–61?
Coll. 21 Dec. 1320 (*Reg. Orleton* p. 386). Resident until 25 March × 23 June 1361 (HCA R438). Also preb. of Preston.

Robert Yve ?1361–9
First occ. 24 June × 28 Sept. 1361 (HCA R438). D. by 3 Aug. 1369 (*CPR 1367–70* pp. 294–5).

Roger Withington 1369–78?
Royal gr. 3 Aug. 1369 (*CPR 1367–70* pp. 294–5). Occ. 29 Sept. × 31 Dec. 1372 (HCA R440). Last occ. 1 Jan. × 24 March 1378 (HCA R444).

John Lanwaryn ?1379–82
First occ. 29 Sept. × 31 Dec. 1379 (HCA R445; *Reg. Gilbert* p. 139). Exch. this preb. 5 Nov. 1382 with Walter Pryde for ch. of Pembridge, Herefs. (*CPR 1381–5* p. 181). But Lanwaryn occ. as can. 11 July 1383 (HCA 2893).

M. Walter Pryde 1382–94
By exch. Nov. 1382. Occ. 24 June × 28 Sept. 1383 (HCA R447). Exch. 13 Oct. 1394 with Nicholas Bridport for a preb. in Pontesbury colleg. ch., Salop. (*Reg. Trefnant* p. 189).

M. Nicholas Bridport 1394–?
By exch. Oct. 1394. Occ. as can. 26 March 1399 (*Reg. Trefnant* p. 158).

Hugh Harper ?–1415
Occ. 25 July 1404 (HCA 1852). D. by 2 Sept. 1415 (*Reg. Mascall* p. 180).

M. John Castell BCL 1415–30
Coll. 2 Sept. 1415 (*Reg. Mascall* p. 180). D. by 7 Nov. 1430 (*Reg. Spofford* p. 357). Also treas. Biog. ref.: *BRUO* I 368.

M. Richard Rotherham 1430–47?
Coll. 7 Nov. 1430 (*Reg. Spofford* p. 357). Last occ. 29 Sept. 1446 × 28 Sept. 1447 (HCA R485). Also treas., chanc. and preb. of Huntington. Biog. ref.: *BRUO* III 1953.

M. John Dylew or **Dellow** BCn&CL ?1448/9–60
Occ. 29 Sept. 1448 × 28 Sept. 1449 (HCA R486). D. by 6 July 1460 (*Reg. Stanbury* p. 176). Also chanc. and unidentified preb. Biog. ref.: *BRUO* I 566–7.

M. John Baily BCL 1460–4
Coll. 7 July 1460 (*Reg. Stanbury* p. 176). Preb. Warham 1464 (*ibid.* p. 180). Also prec. and preb. of Ewithington and Warham. Biog. ref.: *BRUO* I 91.

Thomas Downe 1464–8
Coll. 13 Apr. 1464 (*Reg. Stanbury* p. 179). Exch. 20 July 1468 with Walter Petewynne for preb. of Wellington (*ibid.* p. 192). Also prec.

M. Walter Petewynne DTh 1468–70

By exch. July 1468. D. 4 March 1469 × 11 Apr. 1470 (TNA, PROB 11/6; *Reg. Stanbury* p. 186). Also preb. of Wellington. Biog. ref.: *BRUO* III 1475.

M. John Heynes BCnL 1470–80

Coll. 11 Apr. 1470 (*Reg. Stanbury* p. 186). D. by 6 June 1480 (*Reg. Myllyng* p. 190).

M. John Leche MA 1480–90/1

Coll. 6 June 1480 (*Reg. Myllyng* p. 190). Last occ. as can. 29 Sept. 1490 × 28 Sept. 1491 (HCA R528). Biog. ref.: *BRUO* II 1120.

M. Robert Kent DTh 1491/2?–92/3?

Occ. as can. 29 Sept. 1486 × 28 Sept. 1487 (HCA R524). Fully resident 29 Sept. 1491 × 28 Sept. 1492 and 29 Sept. 1492 × 28 Sept. 1493 in accordance with requirements for the penitentiary (HCA R529–30). Occ. as penitentiary in Mayew's episcopate, 1504 × 1516 (*Reg. Mayew* p. 234). Prec. by 29 Sept. 1496 × 28 Sept. 1497 (HCA R536). D. this preb. 24 Aug. 1515 × 15 Oct. 1515 (TNA, PROB 11/18). Biog. ref.: *BRUO* II 1037.

M. William Porter BTh 1515–24

Coll. 14 Nov. 1515 (*Reg. Mayew* p. 284) and instal. Nov. (HCA 7031/1 fo. 7v). D. 5 Nov. 1524 (*Reg. Booth* p. 338). Also prec. Biog. ref.: *BRUO* III 1503.

M. Rowland Philippes LicTh 1524–31

Coll. 6 Nov. 1524 (*Reg. Booth* p. 338). Instal. in person 17 Nov. (HCA 7031/1 fo. 36). Res. by 7 Apr. 1531 (*Reg. Booth* p. 345). Also prec. Biog. ref.: *BRUO* III 1477–8; J. P. D. Cooper, 'Philipps, Rowland (1467/8–1538?)', *ODNB* <http://www.oxforddnb.com/view/article/22132>.

M. Thomas Parker DCnL 1531

Coll. 7 Apr. 1531 (*Reg. Booth* p. 345). Instal. s.d. (HCA 7031/1 fo. 66v). Exch. 21 July with John Wodrofe for preb. Huntington (*Reg. Booth* p. 345). Also prec. Biog. ref.: *BRUO 1500–40* p. 433.

M. John Wodrofe 1531–3

By exch. July 1531. Instal. 21 July (HCA 7031/1 fo. 67r). D. 1 July × 6 Sept. 1533 (HCA 7031/1 fo. 71; *Reg. Booth* p. 347). Also preb. of Huntington and Moreton and Whaddon. Biog. ref.: *BRUC* p. 647.

M. Walter Mey BTh 1533–58

Coll. 6 Sept. 1533 (*Reg. Booth* p. 347). Instal. 20 Sept. (HCA 7031/1 fo. 71v). D. 17 Sept. × 22 Oct. 1558 (TNA, PROB 11/42a; HCA 7031/1 fo. 152v). Also preb. of Warham. Biog. ref.: *BRUO 1500–40* p. 392.

PREBENDARIES OF EWITHINGTON

The endowment of this preb. was four bovates of land and a watermill in the hamlet of Ewithington or East Withington, in the parish of Withington, Herefs., which was valued at £10 in 1291, 12m in 1294 and £11 6s 8d in 1535 (*Survey of Cath.* I 567; *Taxatio* p. 169b; *Reg. Swinfield* p. 305; *Valor* III 10).

M. William de St John 1277–1316
Coll. 4 Jan. 1277 (*Reg. Cantilupe* p. 121). Renounced canonical house by 29 March 1314 and d. as preb. by 24 Aug. 1316 (*Reg. Swinfield* pp. 544, 547). Biog. ref.: *BRUO* III 1627.

M. Richard de Hamenasch 1316–24
Coll. 24 Aug. 1316 (*Reg. Swinfield* p. 544). D. by 25 Apr. 1324 (*Reg. Orleton* p. 388).

M. Thomas de Astley 1324–49
Robert de Wodehouse 1324–5
Coll. to Astley 25 Apr. 1324 (*Reg. Orleton* p. 388). Royal gr. 29 Apr. to Wodehouse (*CPR 1321–4* p. 407); therefore bp. Orleton asked chapt. 6 May to adm. Astley at once (*Reg. Orleton* p. 326). 18 Apr. 1325, royal revocation of Wodehouse's gr., and gr. to Astley (*CPR 1324–7* p. 112). Astley d. by 31 Aug. 1349 (*Reg. Trillek* p. 380). Biog. ref.: Astley, *BRUO* I 65–6.

Peter Gildesburgh 1349–50
Edmund de Grimsby 1349–54
Prov. to Gildesburgh 28 May 1349 (*CPL* III 314). Royal gr. to Grimsby 22 Aug. (*CPR 1348–50* p. 377; *Reg. Trillek* p. 44). Gildesburgh renounced rights 22 Jan. 1350 (*CCR 1349–54* p. 152; *CPR 1348–50* p. 468). Grimsby occ. as can. 29 Sept. × 31 Dec. 1353 (HCA R433). D. as preb. by 24 Sept. 1354 (*L&G* p. 194n). Biog. ref.: Gildesburgh, A. H. Thompson, 'Pluralism in the medieval church; with notes on pluralists in the diocese of Lincoln, 1366', *Associated Architectural and Archaeological Reports and Papers*, xxxv (1919–20) 199–201.

M. Thomas Griffin of Withrington ?1354–?
Prov. 24 Sept. 1354 (*L&G* p. 98; *CPL* III 518). Occ. as can. 24 June × 28 Sept. 1357 and this preb. 20 Oct. 1358 (HCA R435; *CPR 1354–61* p. 529).

Thomas Brantingham 1361–70
Royal gr. 21 Oct. 1361 (*CPR 1361–4* p. 100). Bp. of Exeter 1370. Elected bp. of Hereford. Biog. ref.: R. G. Davies, 'Brantingham, Thomas (d. 1394)', *ODNB* <http://www.oxforddnb.com/view/article/3278>.

M. Nicholas Long 1370–5
Prov. to Long on el. of Brantingham to see of Exeter 5 Apr. 1370 (*L&G* p. 406). Exch. this preb. 20 Feb. 1375 with William de Humberston for wardenship of Northburgh chantry in St Paul's, London (*Reg. Courtenay* p. 14).

M. William de Humberston or **Humbleton** 1375–?

Prov. to this preb. 21 Nov. 1369 (*L&G* p. 496). By exch. Feb. 1375. Occ. 7 Nov. 1393 (*Reg. Trefnant* pp. 56–7). Also preb. of Moreton Parva.

John Hayward ?1395

Estate as preb. ratif. 24 Feb. 1395; revoked 8 March (*CPR 1391–6* pp. 550, 560).

John Elvet 1395–?

Coll. 11 June 1395 (*Reg. Trefnant* p. 179). Occ. 8 Nov. 1399 (*CPR 1399–1401* p. 54).

M. Henry Hamertone ?–1402

Res. this preb. by 29 Nov. 1402 (*Reg. Trefnant* p. 185). Biog. ref.: *BRUC* p. 283.

John Hartlepool 1402–32

Coll. 29 Nov. 1402 (*Reg. Trefnant* p. 185). D. Nov 1432, m.i. Sandy, Beds. (*Survey of Cath.* I 567). Biog. ref.: Richardson, *Chancery* pp. 75–7.

Robert Parfit 1432–48

Coll. 4 Dec. 1432 (*Reg. Spofford* p. 358). Exch. 18 Aug. 1448 with Nicholas Caraunt for ch. of Symondsbury, Dors. (*The Register of Thomas Beckynton, Bishop of Bath and Wells, 1443–65*, ed. H. C. Maxwell-Lyte and M. C. B. Dawes (Somerset Record Soc., xlix–l, 1934–5) I 100).

M. Nicholas Caraunt LicCL 1448–53

By exch. Aug. 1448. Res. by 1 March 1453 (*Reg. Stanbury* p. 173). Biog. ref.: *BRUO* I 353.

John Barbour 1453–55

Coll. 1 March 1453 (*Reg. Stanbury* p. 173). D. by 29 Oct. 1455 (*ibid.* p. 174).

John Persons 1455–66

Coll. 29 Oct. 1455 (*Reg. Stanbury* p. 174). Preb. Bartonsham 1466.

M. John Baily BCL 1466–79

Coll. 2 Apr. 1466 (*Reg. Stanbury* p. 182). D. 5 July × 8 Sept. 1479 (HCA R369; *Reg. Myllyng* p. 189). Also prec. and preb. of Episcopi and Warham. Biog. ref.: *BRUO* I 91.

M. Richard Jaquessone BCnL 1479–97

Coll. 17 Sept. 1479 (*Reg. Myllyng* p. 189). D. 23 Nov. 1497 m.i. Hereford cath. (*Survey of Cath.* I 568). Also preb. of Hunderton. Biog. ref.: *BRUO* II 1011.

Ranulph Pole ?1507/8–38

Occ. as can. 29 Sept. 1507 × 28 Sept. 1508 (HCA R548). Occ. this 29 Dec. 1515 (*CPL* XX no. 427). D. as preb. 12 March × 13 Apr. 1538 (TNA, PROB 11/27; HCA 7031/1 fo. 81). Biog. ref.: *BRUO 1500–40* p. 696.

M. William Buckmaster DTh 1538–45

Instal. 13 Apr. 1538 (HCA 7031/1 fo. 81r). D. by 14 Sept. 1545 (London, GL MS. 9531/12 fo. 153r; HRO, AL 19/14 fo. 64r). Biog. ref.: S. Wright, 'Buckmaster, William (d. 1546)', *ODNB* <http://www.oxforddnb.com/view/article/3873>.

PREBENDARIES OF GORWELL AND OVERBURY

The endowment of this preb., known as Woolhope in the medieval period, was a carucate of land and rents in Woolhope and four bovates in Gorwell, in Canon Pyon, Herefs. In the 1291 *Taxatio* there are two valuations – Woolhope and Gorwell, £5 9s 8d; and a second one for Gorwell of £2 10s – but both were held by the same person (*Taxatio* pp. 169b, 170a). In 1294 the preb. was valued at 10m and in 1535 at £8 8s 9½d (*Fasti Hereford 1066–1300* pp. 38–9; *Reg. Swinfield* p. 154; *Valor* III 11).

William de Mortimer ?1290/1–1300

Occ. as can. 25 Sept. 1287, and this preb. 1291 (*Reg. Swinfield* p. 154; *Taxatio* pp. 169b, 170a). Preb. Cublington 1300.

M. John of Winchelsea MA 1300–?

Coll. to preb. Woolhope 15 Jan. 1300 (*Reg. Swinfield* p. 532). Preb. Moreton and Whaddon 1312. Biog. ref.: *BRUO* III 2056–7.

M. Michael de Berham DCL ?1313/14–20?

Occ. as can. 29 Sept. 1313 × 28 Sept. 1314 (HCA R401), and this preb. 23 Nov. 1318 (HCA 2799). Last occ. as can. 30 Apr. 1319 (HCA 2994). Probably to d. by 2 Oct. 1320 (*The Register of Walter Stapeldon, Bishop of Exeter 1307–26*, ed. F. C. Hingeston-Randolph (1886) p. 205). Also preb. of Putson Major. Biog. ref.: *BRUO* III 2151.

Adam Osger or **Esgar** 1341–75
Henry Wakefield 1369
Betrand Lagier OFM, DTh, card. bp. of Ostia 1372

Coll. to Osger 4 June 1341 (*Reg. T. Charlton* p. 82). Osger occ. as can. 26 June 1375 (HCA 1762). Royal gr. to Wakefield 21 Dec. 1369 (*CPR 1367–70* p. 340) but Osger in account rolls until 1375. Prov. of this preb. to Lagier with chancellorship 23 Sept. 1372 (*L&G* p. 496). Biog. ref.: Wakefield, R. G. Davies, 'Wakefield, Henry (c.1335–95)', *ODNB* <http://www.oxforddnb.com/view/article/37532; Lagier, C. Berton, *Dictionnaire des cardinaux* (Paris, 1857) pp. 117–18.

M. Adam Robelyn BCnL 1375–?

Bp.'s mand. adm. 5 Dec. 1375 (HCA 2783). Occ. 29 Sept. 1379 × 28 Sept. 1380 (HCA R445). Still alive 8 June 1383, and preb.? (J. Le Neve, *Fasti Ecclesiae Anglicanae 1300–1541*, xi: *Welsh Dioceses*, comp. B. Jones (1965) p. 60).

M. John Prat 1390–1416

Coll. 25 Sept. 1390 (*Reg. Trefnant* p. 174). D. 10 March 1416 (*Survey of Cath.* I 572; *Reg. Mascall* p. 181).

Robert Felton 1416–33
Coll. 23 Apr. 1416 (*Reg. Mascall* p. 181). Res. by 1 May 1433 (*Reg. Spofford* p. 359). Also prec.

M. Thomas Mordon or **Sottewell** BCL 1433–58
Coll. 1 May 1433 (*Reg. Spofford* p. 359). D. 30 Apr. 1458 m.i. Fladbury, Worcs. Biog. ref.: *BRUO* II 1301–2.

M. Thomas Manning BCnL 1458–9
Coll. 31 May 1458 (*Reg. Stanbury* p. 175). Preb. of Colwall 1459. Biog. ref.: *BRUO* II 1216–17.

M. John Grene or **Holder** BCL 1459–63
Coll. 22 May 1459 (*Reg. Stanbury* p. 176). Preb. of Bullinghope 1463. Also preb. of Hampton. Biog. ref.: *BRUO* II 819.

Hugh Ragon 1463–?
Coll. 4 Dec. 1463 (*Reg. Stanbury* p. 179). Occ. as can. continuously from 29 Sept. 1463 × 28 Sept. 1464 until 29 Sept. 1501 × 28 Sept. 1502 (HCA R500–41). Can. unidentified preb. 1471/2–1501/2. Also preb. of Pratum Majus and Withington Parva.

William de la Cova ?1471/2–5
Occ. as can. 29 Sept. 1471 × 28 Sept. 1472 (HCA R508). D. as preb. by 6 Apr. 1475 (*Reg. Myllyng* p. 185).

M. John Pykyng MA 1475–82
Coll. 6 April 1475 (*Reg. Myllyng* p. 185). Exch. 18 July 1482 with Robert Keynell for ch. St Botolph, London (*ibid.* p. 202). Biog. ref.: *BRUC* p. 466.

M. Robert Keynell DCnL 1482–3?
By exch. July 1482. D. by 28 May 1483, as preb.? (Lincolnshire Archives Office, Reg. XXII fo. 223v). Biog. ref.: *BRUO* I 376.

M. John Vaughan BCnL 1483–5
Coll. 1 Sept. 1483 (*Reg. Myllyng* p. 193). D. by 16 Dec. 1485 (*ibid.* p. 194). Biog. ref.: *BRUO* III 1941.

M. Thomas Chaundler DTh 1485–90
Coll. 16 Dec. 1485 (*Reg. Myllyng* p. 194). D. 2 Nov. 1490 (*ibid.* p. 198). Also dean and preb. of Pratum Majus. Biog. ref.: *BRUO* I 398–9; J. Catto, 'Chaundler, Thomas (*c.*1417–90)', *ODNB* <http://www.oxforddnb.com/view/article/5200>.

M. John Nans DCn&CL 1490–1508
Coll. 2 Nov. 1490 (*Reg. Myllyng* p. 198). D. 26 July × 17 Sept. 1508 (*Calendar of the Manuscripts of the Dean and Chapter of Wells*, ed. W. H. B. Bird and W. P. Baildon (2 vols., Historical Manuscripts Commission,

1907–14) II 209; Devon RO, Chanter MS. 13 fo. 25v). Also preb. of Putson Minor. Biog. ref.: *BRUO* II 1336–7.

M. William Webbe MA 1508
Coll. 26 Sept. 1508 (*Reg. Mayew* p. 276). Preb. of Wellington Oct. 1508. Also archdcn. of Hereford and Shropshire and preb. of Inkberrow and Moreton Magna. Biog. ref.: *BRUO* III 2004.

M. Henry Martin BCn&CL 1508–12
Coll. 31 Dec. 1508 (*Reg. Mayew* p. 276). Preb. of Wellington 1512. Also archdcn. of Hereford and Shropshire and preb. of Inkberrow, Norton, Warham and Withington Parva. Biog. ref.: *BRUO* II 1234.

M. Hugh Pole MA 1512–26
Coll. 16 June 1512 (*Reg. Mayew* p. 280). Preb. of Moreton and Whaddon 1526. Also treas. and preb. of Hinton and Norton. Biog. ref.: *BRUO* II 1490.

M. John Cragge MA 1526–53
Coll. 6 Sept. 1526 (*Reg. Booth* p. 339). Instal. 7 Sept. (HCA 7031/1 fo. 38r). D. by 6 March 1553 (TNA, PROB 11/36). Also preb. of Pratum Majus. Biog. ref.: *BRUO 1500–40* p. 148.

PREBENDARIES OF HAMPTON

The endowment of this preb. was land in the parish of Hampton Bishop, Herefs., which was valued at £1 7s 8d in 1291, 2m in 1294 and £2 12s in 1535 (*Survey of Cath.* I 573; *Taxatio* p. 169a; *Reg. Swinfield* p. 305; *Valor* III 11).

John Pole ?1292/3–1304
Occ. as can. 29 Sept. 1292 × 28 Sept. 1293 and subsequently until 1304 (HCA R384–90). D. as preb. by 23 Feb. 1304 (*Reg. Swinfield* p. 535).

M. Simon Faversham DTh 1304–6
Coll. 23 Feb. 1304 (*Reg. Swinfield* p. 535). D. 24 May × 20 July 1306 (*CPR 1301–7* p. 435; *Reg. Clement V* no. 1492). Biog. ref.: *BRUO* II 672.

Walter de Chilton 1306–?
Prov. to preb. of Simon Faversham 20 July 1306 (*Reg. Clement V* no. 1492).

James Henley ?1311–30
Occ. as can. 24 June × 28 Sept. 1311 and 17 Dec. 1315 (HCA R398, 1848). D. as preb. by 25 Sept. 1330 (*Reg. T. Charlton* p. 76).

Thomas Hacluit 1330–75
Expect. 24 Apr. 1326 and still expect. 13 March 1330 (*CPL* II 253, 307). Coll. 25 Sept. 1330 (*Reg. T. Charlton* p. 76). Occ. 25 March × 23 June 1374 and d. 1375,

probably by 29 Sept. 1375 and certainly by 11 March 1376 (*Reg. Gilbert* p. 107; HCA R442; *L&G* p. 497). Also chanc.

John Bridwode 1375–88?

Expect. 26 March 1371 (*L&G* pp. 424, 497; *Lettres Gregoire XI* no. 8396). Occ. as can. 29 Sept. × 31 Dec. 1375 (HCA R442). Last occ. 24 June × 28 Sept. 1388 (HCA R452).

Hugh Vaughan ?1389–1404

Occ. as can. 29 Sept. × 31 Dec. 1389 (HCA R453). Occ. this preb. 9 Feb. 1391 (*CPR 1388–91* p. 375). Exch. by 4 Aug. 1404 with Richard Dyer for ch. of Swinden, Glos. (*CPR 1401–5* p. 415).

M. Richard Dyer 1404–19

Royal gr. 4 Aug. 1404 after exch. Res. by 22 Feb. 1419 (*Reg. Lacy H* p. 115).

M. John Grene or **Holder** BCL 1419–59

Coll. 22 Feb. 1419 (*Reg. Lacy H* p. 115). Preb. of Gorwell and Overbury 1459. Also preb. of Bullinghope. Biog. ref.: *BRUO* II 819.

Robert Catesby BA 1459–81

Coll. 1 Aug. 1459 (*Reg. Stanbury* p. 176). Res. by 3 March 1481 (*Reg. Myllyng* p. 191).

John Burline 1481–?

Coll. 3 Aug. 1481 (*Reg. Myllyng* p. 191).

M. Thomas Alcock ?1503/4–23

Occ. as can. 29 Sept. 1503 × 28 Sept. 1504 (HCA R544). Res. by 18 March 1523 (*Reg. Booth* p. 335). Biog. ref.: *BRUC* pp. 6–7.

M. John Prynne DCnL 1523–51

Coll. 18 March 1523 (*Reg. Booth* p. 335). Occ. on pardon roll 28 Nov. 1547 (*CPR 1548–9* p. 149). Res. by 21 Nov. 1551 (HRO, AL 19/14 fo. 85v). Biog. ref.: *BRUO 1500–40* pp. 465–6.

PREBENDARIES OF HINTON

The endowment of this preb. was a carucate of land, together with rents, pleas and perquisites in the parish of St Martin's, Hereford, which was valued at £5 6s 8d in 1291, 12m in 1294 and £7 9s 10d in 1535 (*Survey of Cath.* I 574; *Fasti Hereford 1066–1300* p. 41; *Taxatio* p. 169a; *Reg. Swinfield* p. 305; *Valor* III 10).

M. Roger of Canterbury 1299

Coll. 4 Aug. 1299 (*Reg. Swinfield* p. 531). Preb. of Preston Nov. 1299. Also treas., archdcn. of Shropshire and preb. of Wellington.

M. Thomas de Lugoure DCL ?1299/1300–13

Bp. excuses his inability to gr. him a preb. 8 Oct. 1292 (*Reg. Swinfield* p. 542). Occ. as can. 29 Sept. 1299 × 28 Sept. 1300 (HCA R389). D. as preb. by 3 Nov. 1313 (*Reg. Swinfield* p. 542). Biog. ref.: *BRUO* II 1174–5.

Stephen de Thaneto 1313–16

Coll. 3 Nov. 1313 (*Reg. Swinfield* p. 542). Occ. as can. 10 Jan. 1316 (*ibid.* p. 505) and d. by 4 June 1317 (HCA 2072).

M. William Knapton DCL 1316–18

Coll. 7 June 1316, by virtue of gr. by abp. Reynolds (*Reg. Swinfield* pp. 513–14; HCA 3155). Depriv. by bp. 18 Oct. 1318 (*Reg. Orleton* pp. 79, 84). Biog. ref.: *BRUC* p. 340.

M. Gilbert de Middleton 1318–30

Coll. 18 Oct. 1318 (*Reg. Orleton* p. 79). Bp.'s mand. adm. 13 Nov. (*ibid.* p. 84). D. 8 Dec. 1330 × 1 Jan. 1331 (*CPR 1330–4* p. 19; *CPL* II 500). Biog. ref.: *BRUO* II 1274–5.

Laurence de St Maur 1335–7

Coll. 24 Aug. 1335 (*Reg. T. Charlton* p. 79). Probably to d. by 14 May 1337 (Lincoln, *The Registers of Henry Burghersh, 1320–42,* ed. N. Bennett (2 vols., Lincoln Record Soc., lxxxvii, xc, 1999–2003) II no. 1569).

M. Itherius de Concoreto BCn&CL ?1337–?

Prov. 20 Feb. 1331 (*CPL* II 327). Occ. 3 Aug. 1337 (*CPR 1334–8* p. 487). Had married by 15 June 1343 (*CPP* p. 57).

M. John Rees DCnL ?1340–53
William de Herlaston 1350

Rees occ. as can. 24 June × 28 Sept. 1340 (HCA R425) and this preb. 23 Nov. 1350 (*CPR 1350–4* p. 12). Royal gr. to Herlaston 25 June 1350 (*CPR 1348–50* p. 538) but ineffective. Rees d. by 3 March 1353 (*Reg. Trillek* p. 386). Herlaston also preb. of Hunderton.

Nicholas Kaerwent 1353–81

Expect. 20 June 1343 (*CPL* III 98). Coll. 3 March 1353 (*Reg. Trillek* p. 386). Conf. by pope 28 July 1353 (*CPL* III 477; *CPP* p. 251). Occ 13 Nov. 1366 (Cant., *Reg. Langham* p. 13). Probably to d. 7 Apr. 1381 (Winchester, *Reg. Wykeham* I 117–18).

David ap Jake ?1381–96

Occ. as can. 29 Sept. × 31 Dec. 1381 (HCA R446). D. as preb. 24 Sept. 1396 (*Reg. Trefnant* p. 181).

M. Reginald Wolstone BCnL 1396–1411

Coll. 24 Sept. 1396 (*Reg. Trefnant* p. 181). Estate ratif. 10 Feb. 1397 (*CPR 1396–9* p. 68; HCA 766). D. by 24 Aug. 1411 (*Reg. Mascall* p. 177). Also preb. of Norton.

John Baily 1411–12
   Coll. 24 Aug. 1411 (*Reg. Mascall* p. 177). D. 21 × 25 Sept. 1412 (TNA, PROB 11/2A; *Reg. Mascall* p. 178).

M. Edmund Lacy DTh 1412–17
   Coll. 25 Sept. 1412 (*Reg. Mascall* p. 178). Bp. of Hereford 1417. Biog. ref.: *BRUO* II 1081–3; Nicholas Orme, 'Lacy, Edmund (*c.*1370–1455)', *ODNB* <http://www.oxforddnb.com/view/article/15846>.

Thomas Morton 1419–?
   Coll. 19 Apr. 1419 (*Reg. Lacy H* p. 3). Occ as can. 29 Sept. 1420 × 28 Sept. 1421 (HCA R472). D. 10 Jan. 1448 × 28 May 1449, as can.? (*Testamenta Eboracensis* III, ed. J. Raine (Surtees Soc., xlv, 1865) pp. 106–7).

Thomas Woodford or **Belton** ?–1452
   D. as preb. by 8 Apr. 1452 (*Reg. Boulers* p. 22; J. Le Neve, *Fasti Ecclesiae Anglicanae 1300–1541*, v: *St Paul's*, comp. J. M. Horn (1964) p. 63). Biog. ref.: *Lincoln Visitations* I 206–7.

M. Richard Pede DCnL 1452–8
   Coll. 25 Apr. 1452 (*Reg. Boulers* p. 22). Preb. of Moreton Magna 1458. Also dean., treas. and preb. of Huntington. Biog. ref.: *BRUO* II 1449–50.

M. Robert Dobbys DCnL 1458–60
   Coll. 7 Dec. 1458 (*Reg. Stanbury* p. 175). Res. by 5 March 1460 (*ibid.* p. 176). Biog. ref.: *BRUO* I 579–80.

M. John Clone 1460–5
   Coll. 5 March 1460 (*Reg. Stanbury* p. 176). D. by 16 Aug. 1465 (*ibid.* p. 181). Also preb. of Pratum Minus.

M. Robert Dobbys DCnL (again) 1465–76
   Coll. 5 Oct. 1465 (*Reg. Stanbury* p. 181). D. by 21 Apr. 1476 (*Reg. Myllyng* p. 186). Biog. ref.: *BRUO* I 579–80.

M. Thomas Morton BCL 1476–1511
   Coll. 21 Apr. 1476 (*Reg. Myllyng* p. 186). D. 25 June × 20 July 1511 (TNA, PROB 11/17; *Reg. Mayew* p. 278). Also archdcn. of Hereford and Shropshire. Biog. ref.: *BRUO* II 1321–2.

M. Hugh Pole MA 1511–12
   Coll. 20 July 1511 (*Reg. Mayew* p. 278). Preb. Gorwell and Overbury 1512. Also treas. and preb. of Moreton and Whaddon and Norton. Biog. ref.: *BRUO* II 1490.

John Olyver or **Smythe** 1512–58
   Coll. 15 July 1512 (*Reg. Mayew* p. 280). Occ. 29 Oct. 1557 (*CPR 1557–8* p. 355). D. 19 Nov. × 2 Dec. 1558 (HCA 7031/1 fos. 152v–153r). Also preb. of Norton. Biog. ref.: *BRUO 1500–40* p. 425.

PREBENDARIES OF HUNDERTON

The endowment of this preb. was a carucate of land and rents in Hunderton, in Clehonger, Herefs., and the parish of St John Baptist, Hereford which was valued at £5 8s in 1291, 100s in 1294 and £6 7s 8d in 1535 (*Survey of Cath.* I 576; *Taxatio* p. 169; *Reg. Swinfield* p. 305; *Valor* III 10).

M. Robert of Gloucester or le Wyse 1283–1304

Occ as can. 1277 × 1282 and 26 Dec. 1279 (*Fasti Hereford 1066–1300* pp. 43–4). Coll. this preb. 24 March 1283 (*Reg. Swinfield* pp. 5–6). Preb. of Huntington by 31 Aug. 1304 (*Reg. Swinfield* p. 536). Also chanc. Biog. ref.: *BRUO* II 773–4.

M. Gilbert Segrave ?1304/5–13

Occ. as can. 29 Sept. 1304 × 28 Sept. 1305 (HCA R390). Res. this preb. to become bp. of London 1313. Biog. ref.: *BRUC* p. 516.

M. Robert Icklesham 1313–22

Coll. 26 Nov. 1313 (*Reg. Swinfield* p. 542). D. by 19 Aug. 1322 (*Reg. Orleton* p. 388). Biog. ref.: *BRUO* II 997.

Walter Karles 1322–49

Coll. 19 Aug. 1322 (*Reg. Orleton* p. 388). Instal. 24 Aug. (HCA 832). D. by 3 July 1349 (*L&G* p. 110).

Roger Braynton 1349–51
Nicholas Hethe 1349–63
William de Herlaston 1351–6
M. Henry de Shipton 1356

Prov. to Braynton of larger preb. though he already had a smaller one, Norton, 19 June 1343 (*CPL* III 99). Prov. to Hethe 4 July 1349 (*CPL* III 319). Braynton occupied this preb. on d. of Karles and paid Hethe to allow him to keep it (*Reg. Trillek* pp. 244–5). Royal gr. to Herlaston 9 July 1351 on d. of Braynton (*CPR 1350–4* p. 148), and prohibns. against Hethe 10 Feb. 1352 (*ibid.* pp. 277–8). Bp.'s mand. adm. Herlaston 20 Feb. (*Reg. Trillek* pp. 44–5); d. by 10 Nov. 1356 (*ibid.* pp. 244–5). Coll. to Shipton 16 Nov. 1356 (*ibid.* pp. 389, 244–5), but Hethe gained possession and occ. 1 Jan. × 24 March 1361 and 24 June × 28 Sept. 1362 (HCA R438–9). Res. 24 Dec. 1363 (*Reg. L. Charlton* p. 23), but said to have been depriv. by pope for plurality by 30 Aug. 1364 (*L&G* p. 252). Braynton also preb. of Wellington; Herlaston claimed preb. of Hinton; Hethe also preb. of Bullinghope; Shipton also prec., treas., archdcn. of Shropshire and preb. of Putson Minor. Biog. ref.: Hethe, *BRUC* p. 302.

M. Roger Otery BCL 1363–?
M. Nicholas Drayton BCL 1366
Richard de la Mere 1370

Coll. to Otery 24 Dec. 1363 (*Reg. L. Charlton* pp. 23, 66). K. recovered right of pres. against Hethe 16 Nov. 1364 and 25 July 1365 (*CPR 1364–7* pp. 73, 202).

Bp.'s mand. to adm. Otery 9 Apr. 1366 (*Reg. L. Charlton* p. 23). Prov to Drayton 30 Aug. 1364 after depriv. of Hethe and again 29 Aug. 1366 but said to be ineffective by 1371 × 1374 (*L&G* pp. 252, 289, 381). Otery still litigating for possession 18 Nov. 1366 (Cant., *Reg. Langham* pp. 44–5). Royal gr. to him 3 Nov. 1369 (*CPR 1367–70* p. 317). Royal gr. to Mere 24 Nov. 1370 (*CPR 1370–4* p. 21) but doubtful if he gained possession. Chapt. gr. costs of Mere's litigation 25 Nov. 1376 (*Ch. & Rec.* p. 238). Otery occ. as can. 29 Sept. × 31 Dec. 1375 (HCA R443). Biog. ref.: Otery, *BRUO* II 1409; Drayton, *BRUC* p. 194; A. B. Cobban, 'Drayton, Nicholas (d. in or before 1379)', *ODNB* <http://www.oxforddnb.com/view/article/8043>.

William Ashton 1376–?
Royal gr. 21 Jan. 1376 (*CPR 1374–7* p. 216). Occ. as can. 24 June × 28 Sept. 1378 (HCA R444).

Henry Buyton ?1383–1412
Estate as preb. ratif. 19 March 1377; revoked 4 Apr. (*CPR 1374–7* pp. 440, 442). Occ. as can. 29 Sept. × 31 Dec. 1383 and estate ratif. again 11 Aug. 1387 (HCA R448; *CPR 1385–9* p. 351). D. by 23 Sept. 1412 (*Reg. Mascall* p. 178).

John Walwayn 1412–?
Coll. 23 Sept. 1412 (*Reg. Mascall* p. 178) and occ. as can. 11 Aug. 1415 (*ibid.* p. 85).

Thomas Berkeley ?1416–20
M. William Lyndwood DCn&CL 1420–42
Berkeley occ. as can. 23 Nov. 1416 (Cant., *Reg. Chichele* II 107). Preb. disputed between Berkeley and Lyndwood 9 June 1420 (*ibid.* IV 77, 80). Coll. to Lyndwood 3 Nov. 1423 (*Reg. Spofford* p. 351). Bp. of St Davids 1442. Biog. ref.: Lyndwood, *BRUO* II 1191–3; R. M. Helmholz, 'Lyndwood, William (*c*.1375–1446)', *ODNB* <http://www.oxforddnb.com/view/article/17264>.

M. Andrew Holes DCnL 1442–6
Coll. 4 Sept. 1442 (*Reg. Spofford* p. 364). Res by 9 Apr. 1446 (*ibid.* p. 366). Biog. ref.: *BRUO* II 949–50; J. Hughes, 'Holes, Andrew (d. 1470)', *ODNB* <http://www.oxforddnb.com/view/article/50148>.

M. Robert Tarry BCL 1446–72
Coll. 9 Apr. 1446 (*Reg. Spofford* p. 366). Preb. of Huntington 1472.

M. Richard Jaquessone BCnL 1472–9
Coll. 9 Apr. 1472 (*Reg. Stanbury* p. 188). Preb. of Ewithington 1479. Biog. ref.: *BRUO* II 1011.

M. Robert Ashcombe MA 1479–1528
Robert Huisem 1505
Coll. Sept. 1479 (*Reg. Myllyng* p. 190). A Robert Huisem occ. this preb., or perhaps Huntington?, 25 Nov. 1505 (*CPL* XVIII no. 531). Lic. to Ashcombe to negotiate with William Burghill for a pension when he res. the preb. but ineffective

(*Reg. Mayew* pp. 201–2). Ashcombe d. this preb. by 14 Apr. 1528 (*Reg. Booth* p. 341). Biog. ref.: Ashcombe, *BRUO* I 55.

M. William Edwards 1528–38

Coll. 14 Apr. 1528 (*Reg. Booth* p. 341). Instal. 18 May (HCA 7031/1 fo. 44r). D. by 29 Jan. 1538 (*Reg. Booth* p. 379). Also preb. of Pratum Minus. Biog. ref.: *BRUO 1500–40* p. 676.

M. Hugh Coren or Curwen DCL 1538–52

Coll. 29 Jan. 1538 (*Reg. Booth* p. 379). Instal. 5 Feb. (HCA 7031/1 fo. 80v). Preb. of Bartonsham 1552. Biog. ref.: *BRUO 1500–40* pp. 137–8; H. C. Walshe, 'Curwen, Hugh (*c.*1500–68)', *ODNB* <http://www.oxforddnb.com/view/article/6966>.

PREBENDARIES OF HUNTINGTON

The endowment of this preb. was two carucates of land, rents, a mill and pleas and perquisites in Huntington chapelry in the parish of Holmer, Herefs., which were valued at £9 4s in 1291, 20m in 1294 and £8 19s 10d in 1535 (*Survey of Cath.* I 578; *Taxatio* p. 170a; *Reg. Swinfield* p. 305; *Valor* III 9).

M. John de Bestane 1295–1304

Coll. 13 Aug. 1295 (*Reg. Swinfield* p. 530). D. by 31 Aug. 1304 (*ibid.* p. 536). Biog. ref.: *BRUO* III 2151–2.

M. Robert of Gloucester or le Wyse DCnL 1304–22

Coll. 31 Aug. 1304 (*Reg. Swinfield* p. 536). D. by 31 Jan. 1322 (*Reg. Orleton* p. 387). Also chanc. and preb. of Hunderton. Biog. ref.: *BRUO* II 773–4.

Philip Ilger ?1348–61
William Huntlowe 1354

Expect. to Ilger 7 Nov. 1342 (*CPL* III 80). Occ. as can. 8 Dec. 1348 (*Reg. Trillek* p. 475). Royal gr. to Huntlowe 4 Oct. 1354 (*CPR 1354–8* p. 105) but ineffective? Ilger occ. as can. from 29 Sept. × 31 Dec. 1352 to 24 June × 28 Sept. 1361 (HCA R432–8). Huntlowe preb. Inkberrow 1361.

M. Robert Wycheford 1361–74

Royal gr. 16 Aug. 1361 (*CPR 1361–4* p. 52). Res. 8 Apr. 1374 (*Reg. Gilbert* p. 120).

John Cheyne 1387

Royal gr. 3 March 1387 (*CPR 1385–9* p. 301). Coll. 16 Apr. (*Reg. Gilbert* p. 120). Biog. ref.: *BRUC* pp. 134–5.

Thomas Picton ?1387–?

Occ. 3 Oct. 1387 (*CPR 1385–9* p. 359). Occ. as can. from 25 March × 23 June 1387 to 1 Jan. × 24 March 1388 (HCA R451–2) and 7 Nov. 1393 when called Pylton (*Reg. Trefnant* p. 57).

M. Thomas More ?–1421

Occ. 5 Jan. 1396 (*CPR 1391–6* p. 662). D. 23 Dec. 1421 (J. Le Neve, *Fasti Ecclesiae Anglicanae 1300–1541*, v: *St Paul's*, comp. J. M. Horn (1963) p. 6). Also preb. of Moreton Parva. Biog. ref.: *Reg. Chichele* II 665.

M. Walter Eston LicCL 1421–2

Coll. 29 Dec. 1421 (*Reg. Polton* pp. 11–12). Called *nuper canonicus* 29 Sept. 1422 × 28 Sept. 1423 (HCA R474). Biog. ref.: *BRUC* p. 215.

M. John Langton BCnL 1422–3

Bp.'s mand. adm. 14 Feb. 1422 (HCA 2788). Instal. 8 May (*ibid.*). Res. by 5 March 1423 (HCA 2789). Also preb. of Moreton Parva. Biog. ref.: *BRUC* pp. 351–2.

M. John Nichole or **Sudbury** BTh 1423–?

Bp.'s mand. adm. 5 March 1423; instal. 14 March (HCA 2789). D. by 1 May 1436, as preb.? (*CPR 1429–36* p. 513). Biog. ref.: *BRUC* pp. 565–6.

M. Richard Rotherham DTh ?1447–54

Probably held this preb. after res. preb. of Episcopi in 1446–7. Res. this preb. by 26 Oct. 1454 (*Reg. Stanbury* p. 173). Also chanc. and treas. Biog. ref.: *BRUO* III 1953.

M. Richard Rudhale DCnL 1454–72

Coll. 26 Oct. 1454 (*Reg. Stanbury* p. 173). Preb. of Bullinghope 1472. Also treas. and archdcn. of Hereford. Biog. ref.: *BRUO* III 1603.

M. Robert Tarry BCL 1472–8

Coll. 3 Apr. 1472 (*Reg. Stanbury* p. 188). D. by Feb. 1478 (*Reg. Myllyng* p. 188). Also preb. of Hunderton.

M. Richard Martyn BCnL 1478

Coll. Feb. 1478 (*Reg. Myllyng* p. 188). Exch. 25 July with Richard Pede for preb. of Moreton Magna (*ibid.* p. 202). Also archdcn. of Hereford and preb. of Pratum Minus and Putson Minor. Biog. ref.: *BRUO* II 1236–7; J. Hughes, 'Martyn, Richard (d. 1483)', *ODNB* <http://www.oxforddnb.com/view/article/18236>.

M. Richard Pede DCnL 1478–81

By exch. July 1478. D. by 26 March 1481 (*Reg. Myllyng* p. 62). Also dean, treas. and preb. of Hinton and Moreton Magna. Biog. ref.: *BRUO* III 1449–50.

M. Christopher Twyneho BA ?–1508

Occ. as can. 29 Sept. 1504 × 28 Sept. 1505 (HCA R547). Exch. this preb. Feb. 1508 with John Wodrofe for preb. of Moreton and Whaddon (*Reg. Mayew* p. 275). Biog. ref.: *BRUO* III 1919–20.

M. John Wodrofe 1508–31

By exch. Feb. 1508. Exch. 21 July 1531 with Thomas Parker for preb. of Episcopi (*Reg. Booth* p. 345). Also preb. of Moreton and Whaddon. Biog. ref.: *BRUC* p. 647.

M. Thomas Parker DCnL 1531–8

By exch. July 1531. Instal. 21 July (HCA 7031/1 fo. 67r). D. 22 Sept. 1538 (*L&P* XIII ii no. 491 (19)). Also prec. and preb. of Episcopi. Biog. ref.: *BRUO 1500–40* p. 433.

Richard Benson 1538–49

Pres. by k., patron *sede vacante*, 27 Sept. 1538 (*L&P* XIII ii no. 491 (19); HCA 2793). Instal. 20 Oct. as on royal coll. (HCA 7031/1 fo. 82r). D. 11 Feb. 1549 m.i., Hereford cath. (Havergal, *Mon. Inscr. Heref.* p. 19; HRO, AL 19/14 fo. 75v).[2] Biog. ref.: *BRUO 1500–40* p. 663.

PREBENDARIES OF INKBERROW

The endowment of this preb. was land in and part or all of the tithes of Inkberrow, Worcs., which was valued at £10 in 1291, 16m in 1294 and £15 0s 1d in 1535 (*Survey of Cath.* I 579; *Taxatio* pp. 171a, 217; *Reg. Swinfield* p. 305; *Valor* III 9).

Stephen de Swinfield 1294–?

Coll. 21 Sept. 1294 and inst. 22 Sept. as Stephen de Gravesend (*Register of Godfrey Giffard, 1268–1301*, ed. J. W. Willis-Bund (2 vols., Worcestershire Historical Soc., xv, 1898–1902) II 447).

M. Richard Vernon DCnL 1319–34

Coll. 15 Feb. 1319 (*Reg. Orleton* p. 385). D. 16 July 1334 (Bod. Lib., MS. Ashmole 794 fo. 72v). Biog. ref.: *BRUO* III 1946.

John de la Chambre 1334–45

Expect. 10 July 1329 (*CPL* II 293). Occ. as can. 25 March × 23 June 1334 (HCA R419). Exch. this preb. 14 March 1345 with John Leach for ch. of Mapledurham and chap. of Petersfield, Hants. (*Reg. Trillek* pp. 22–3). Also treas.

M. John Leach DCnL 1345–61

By exch. March 1345. D. by 21 July 1361 (Worcestershire RO, b 716.093-BA.2648/3(iii) fo. 34r). Biog. ref.: *BRUO* II 1118–19.

M. William Lambeth 1361

Adm. by bp. Worcester 21 July 1361 (Worcestershire RO, b 716.093-BA.2648/3(iii) fo. 34r).

William Huntlowe 1361–89

Royal gr. 11 Nov. 1361 (*CPR 1361–4* p. 112). Adm. 12 Dec. 1361 (*The Register of the Diocese of Worcester during the Vacancy of the See, usually called*

---

[2] *Survey of Cath.* I 578–9 misquoted date as 1547 (hence 1548 New Style), perhaps pursuant to the error that his will was proved 22 Feb. 'following', i.e., 1547/8, when in fact it was proved 22 Feb. 1548/9 (TNA, PROB 11/32).

Registrum Sede Vacante, 1301–1435, ed. J. W. Willis-Bund (Worcestershire Historical Soc., viii, 1897) p. 203). Occ. as can. 29 Sept. × 31 Dec. 1361 and regularly until 29 Sept. × 31 Dec. 1389 (HCA R439–53). Also claimed preb. of Huntington.

M. John Trevaur DCn&CL 1389–95

Coll. 20 Nov. 1389 (*Reg. Trefnant* p. 174). Bp. St Asaph 1395. Biog. ref.: *BRUO* III 1898–9.

John Cresset 1395–7
Thomas Butiller 1396

Coll. to Cresset 8 July 1395 of preb. vac. by William Huntlowe (*Reg. Trefnant* p. 179). Royal gr. to Butiller 3 July 1396 of preb. vac. by John Trevaur (*CPR 1396–9* p. 11). Cresset remained in possession, and res. on 11 Apr. 1397 (*Reg. Trefnant* p. 192). Biog. ref.: Butiller, S. L. Ollard, *Fasti Wyndsoriensis: the Deans and Canons of Windsor* (Windsor, 1950) pp. 26–7.

Hugh Holbach 1397–1407

Coll. 11 Apr. 1397 (*Reg. Trefnant* p. 181), and again 19 Dec. 1398 at k.'s nomination (*ibid.* p. 182). Instal. 19 Dec. (HRO, AL/19/7 fo. 45v). Exch. 4 May 1407 with Thomas Staundon for preb. of Timberscombe in Wells (*Reg. Mascall* p. 183). Biog. ref.: *BRUO* II 944–5.

Thomas Staundon 1407–29

By exch. May 1407. D. by 10 July 1429 (*Reg. Spofford* p. 356).

John Burdet 1429–49

Coll. 10 July 1429 (*Reg. Spofford* p. 356). D. by 27 Jan. 1449 (Lamb., Reg. Stafford fo. 99r).

M. John Stokes DCL 1449–66

Coll. 27 Jan. 1449 (Lamb., Reg. Stafford fo. 99r). D. 19 Dec. 1466 × 1 Jan 1467 (TNA, PROB 11/5; *Reg. Stanbury* p. 183). Biog. ref.: *BRUO* III 1782.

M. Robert Geffrey 1467–94

Coll. 1 Jan. 1467 (*Reg. Stanbury* p. 183). D. 16 July 1492 × 23 Sept. 1494 (TNA, PROB 11/10; Worcestershire RO, b 716.093-BA.2648/7(ii) fo. 56v). Also chanc., treas., archdcn. of Hereford and Shropshire and preb. of Preston. Biog. ref.: *BRUO* II 753–4.

M. Richard Gray 1494–?

Coll. 23 Sept. 1494 (Worcestershire RO, b 716.093-BA.2648/7(ii) fo. 56v). Occ. 29 Sept. 1496 × 28 Sept. 1497 (HCA 4328).

M. Stephen Surteis BTh ?–1510

Occ. as can. 29 Sept. 1504 × 28 Sept. 1505 (HCA R547). D. as preb. by 20 Aug. 1510 (*Reg. Mayew* p. 278). Biog. ref.: *BRUC* p. 567.

M. Richard Smythe DCnL 1510–12

Coll. 20 Aug. 1510 (*Reg. Mayew* p. 278). Preb. of Bullinghope 1512. Biog. ref.: *BRUO* III 1718.

M. William Webbe MA 1512

Coll. 20 Aug. 1512 (*Reg. Mayew* p. 280). Preb. of Moreton Magna Oct. 1512. Also archdcn. of Hereford and Shropshire and preb. of Gorwell and Overbury, Moreton Magna and Wellington. Biog. ref.: *BRUO* III 2004.

M. Henry Martin BCn&CL 1512–23/4

Coll. 14 Oct. 1512 (*Reg. Mayew* p. 280). Instal. 16 Nov. (HCA 7031/1 fo. 2r). D. as preb. 30 Sept. 1523 × 28 Jan. 1524 (HCA 7031/1 fo. 33; *Reg. Booth* p. 336). Also archdcn. of Hereford and Shropshire and preb. of Gorwell and Overbury, Norton, Warham and Withington Parva. Biog. ref.: *BRUO* II 1234.

M. John Booth DTh 1524–42

Coll. 28 Jan. 1524 (*Reg. Booth* p. 336). Instal. by proxy 29 Jan. 1524 and again in person 26 Sept. 1527 (HCA 7031/1 fos. 33r, 40v). D. 8 × 14 Aug. 1542 (*L&P* XVII no. 581; HRO, AL 19/14 fo. 42r–v). Also archdcn. of Shropshire. Biog. ref.: *BRUO 1500–40* p. 61.

PREBENDARIES OF MORETON AND WHADDON

The endowment of this preb. was the rectories of Moreton Valence and Whaddon, Glos., which was valued at £13 6s 8d in 1291, 20m in 1294 and £13 6s 8d in 1535 (*Survey of Cath.* I 581; *Taxatio* p. 224a; *Reg. Swinfield* p. 305; *Valor* III 11). The preb. was not entitled to small commons, the only one who did not share in them (*LS* II 58).

Ralph de Hengham 1279–1311

Coll. 28 Oct. 1279 (*Reg. Cantilupe* p. 225). Res. by 20 Feb. 1311, d. 18 May (*Hereford Fasti 1066–1300* pp. 48–9; *Reg. Swinfield* p. 540).

Hamo of Sandwich 1311–12

Coll. 20 Feb. 1311 (*Reg. Swinfield* p. 540). Exch. 22 March 1312, by which he left Moreton and Whaddon and obtained preb. of Putson Major. Michael de Berham left Putson Major and obtained preb. of Woolhope, which soon ceased to be a preb. of Hereford (see *Reg. Swinfield* p. 305n). John de Winchelsea left Woolhope and obtained preb. of Moreton and Whaddon (*ibid.* p. 541).

M. John Winchelsea MA 1312–16

By exch. March 1312. Res. by 6 Sept. 1316 (*Reg. Swinfield* p. 544). Also preb. of Gorwell and Overbury. Biog. ref.: *BRUO* III 2056–7.

M. John Elham BTh 1316–31

Coll. 6 Sept. 1316 (*Reg. Swinfield* p. 544). Occ. July 1318 (*CPL* II 174), probably until d. by 2 Dec. 1331 (*BRUO* I 633–4). Biog. ref.: *BRUO* I 633–4.

M. Roger Aston DCL occ. 1335, 1339

Prov. to canonry and preb. 23 Nov. 1329 (*CPL* II 323). Occ. 31 Aug. 1335 (*Calendar of the Register of Simon de Monacute, Bishop of Worcester 1334–7*, ed. R. M. Haines (Worcestershire Historical Soc., new ser., xv, 1996) no. 1081) and 26 Sept. 1339 (Worcester, *Reg. Bransford* no. 214). Biog. ref.: *BRUO* I 69.

M. Richard de Chaddesley senior DCnL ?–1348

Expect. 5 Oct. 1332 (*CPL* II 372). D. as preb. by 21 Aug. 1348 (*The Register of John de Grandisson, Bishop of Exeter (AD 1327–69), with Some Account of the Episcopate of James de Berkeley (AD 1327)*, ed. F. C. Hingeston Randolph (3 vols., 1894–9) III 1367). Biog. ref.: *BRUO* I 381.

M. William de Herewynton DCL 1348–?

Coll. 27 Aug. 1348 (Worcester, *Reg. Bransford* no. 392). Preb. Withington Parva 1350. Biog. ref.: *BRUO* II 921.

Henry Resthale of Campeden ?–1349

Expect. 9 June 1343, still expect. 9 Oct. 1344 (*CPP* pp. 56, 78; *CPL* III 130). Exch. this preb. 28 Aug. 1349 with Richard de Retford for ch. Newington, Oxon. (*CPR 1348–50* p. 399; *Reg. Trillek* p. 406; *Calendar of Institutions by the Chapter of Canterbury Sede Vacante*, ed. C. E. Woodruff (Kent Records, viii, 1933) p. 91).

M. Richard of Retford DTh 1349–64

By exch. Aug. 1349. Exch. 29 Apr. 1364 with Edmund de Morteyn for preb. of Throckington in York (York, Borthwick Institute, Reg. 11 fo. 56v). Biog. ref.: *BRUO* III 1541–2.

M. Edmund de Morteyn DCL 1364–6

By exch. Apr. 1364. D. 20 Oct. 1364 × 15 Jan. 1366, probably abroad, and may not have obtained preb. (*CPR 1364–7* pp. 30, 193; *BRUO* II 1316). Biog. ref.: *BRUO* II 1316.

M. William Birmingham DTh ?–1368

Occ. 18 Nov. 1366 (Cant., *Reg. Langham* p. 39). Exch. 29 Oct. 1368 with Roger de Sutton for preb. of Eigne (*Reg. L. Charlton* p. 72). Also dean. Biog. ref.: *BRUO* I 177.

M. Roger Sutton DCL 1368–78
Thomas Hervey 1369

Sutton became preb. by exch. Oct. 1368. Royal gr. to Hervey 1 July 1369 (*CPR 1367–70* p. 281), but Sutton d. as preb. 12 Oct. × 23 Nov. 1378 (*BRUC* p. 568). Sutton also archdcn. of Hereford and preb. of Eigne. Biog. ref.: Sutton, *BRUC* p. 568.

M. John Harold BCn&CL 1378–83

Adm. 21 Dec. 1378 by bp. of Worcester (*A Calendar of the Register of Henry Wakefield, Bishop of Worcester, 1375–95*, ed. W. P. Marett (Worcestershire

Historical Soc., new ser., vii, 1972) no. 70). Estate ratif. 29 Dec. 1370 (*CPR 1377–81* p. 294). Preb. of Norton 1383. Also dean and preb. of Bullinghope. Biog. ref.: *BRUO* II 877.

Walter Prene ?–1386
Exch. this preb. 30 March 1386 with Guy Mone for ch. of Saltwood, Kent (*Reg. Gilbert* p. 125).

Guy Mone 1386–96
By exch. March 1386. Res. by 20 Oct. 1396 (*Reg. Trefnant* p. 181).

Walter Cook 1393
Walter Ameny or **Jakes** 1396–9
Prov. to this preb. to Cook by 5 Oct. 1393 (*CPL* IV 445). Coll. to Ameny 20 Oct. 1396 (*Reg. Trefnant* p. 181). Exch. 8 July 1399 with Richard Winchcombe for preb. of Llandogy in Abergwili colleg. ch., Carm. (*ibid.* p. 190).

M. Richard Winchcombe 1399–1404
By exch. July 1399. D. by 17 Nov. 1404 (*Reg. Mascall* p. 168).

M. John Brugge 1404–7
Coll. 17 Nov. 1404 (*Reg. Mascall* p. 168). D. 24 Aug. 1407 (TNA, PROB 11/2A; *Reg. Mascall* p. 172).

M. John Baysham BCnL 1407–12
Coll. 24 Aug. 1407 (*Reg. Mascall* p. 172). Res. by 8 Apr. 1412 (*ibid.* p. 177). Also dean and preb. of Withington Parva. Biog. ref.: *BRUO* I 135–6.

M. Thomas Balding 1412–15
Coll. 8 Apr. 1412 (*Reg. Mascall* p. 177). Res. by 14 Oct. 1415 (*ibid.* p. 180). Biog. ref.: *Lincoln Visitations* I 192.

M. John Baysham BCnL 1415–20
Coll. 14 Oct. 1415 (*Reg. Mascall* p. 180). Preb. of Wellington 1420. Biog. ref.: *BRUO* I 135–6.

M. William Ingram 1420–6
Coll. 16 Sept. 1420 (*Reg. Lacy H* p. 117). Exch. 8 Nov. 1426 with Thomas Burton for preb. of Torleton in Salisbury (*Reg. Spofford* p. 369).

M. Thomas Burton BCn&CL 1426–30
By exch. Nov. 1426. D. by 2 March 1430 (*Reg. Spofford* p. 356). Biog. ref.: *BRUO* I 321.

Nicholas Dixon 1430–?
Coll. 2 March 1430 (*Reg. Spofford* p. 356). Biog. ref.: Thompson, *Lincoln Visitations* I 198–9.

Thomas Ringstede ?–1446

Exch. this preb. 18 July 1446 with John Breton for preb. of Firle in Chichester (*Reg. Spofford* p. 370).

John Breton 1446–65

By exch. July 1446. D. 6 Apr. 1465 m.i. Lincoln cath. (*Survey of Cath.* II 247).

Walter Hunt O.Carm., DTh 1465–79

Coll. 13 June 1465 (*Reg. Stanbury* p. 181). D. 28 Nov. 1479 (*BRUO* II 986–7). Biog. ref.: *BRUO* II 986–7.

M. Adrian de Bardis 1479–80

Coll. 10 Feb. 1479 (*Reg. Myllyng* pp. 189, 190). Res. by 20 Aug. 1480 (*ibid.* p. 191). Also treas. Biog. ref.: *BRUC* p. 36.

M. Oliver Sompnour BCnL 1480–?

Coll. 20 Aug. 1480 (*Reg. Myllyng* p. 191). D. by 17 May 1499, as preb.? (Lincolnshire Archives Office, Reg. XXIII fo. 282v). Biog. ref.: *BRUO* III 1816.

M. John Wodrofe ?–1508

Occ. as can. 29 Sept. 1507 × 28 Sept. 1508 (HCA R548). Exch. this preb. Feb. 1508 with Christopher Twyneho for preb. of Huntington (*Reg. Mayew* p. 275). Also preb. of Episcopi. Biog. ref.: *BRUC* p. 647.

M. Christopher Twyneho BA 1508–9

By exch. Feb. 1508. D. 7 Aug. 1508 × 16 Dec. 1509 (TNA, PROB 11/6; *Reg. Mayew* p. 277). Also preb. of Huntington. Biog. ref.: *BRUO* III 1919–20.

M. William Goberd BA 1509–12

Coll. 16 Dec. 1509 (*Reg. Mayew* p. 277). Res. by 24 May 1512 (*ibid.* p. 279). Also treas., archdcn. of Shropshire and preb. of Piona Parva. Biog. ref.: *BRUO 1500–40* p. 236.

M. William Gray MA 1512–21

Coll. 24 May 1512 (*Reg. Mayew* p. 279). D. 9 × 14 Feb. 1521 (TNA, PROB 11/20; Wiltshire and Swindon RO, Salisbury Diocesan Records, D1/2/14 fo. 89). Biog. ref.: *BRUO* II 825.

M. David Walker BCL 1522–6

Coll. 17 Feb. 1522 (*Reg. Booth* p. 334). Instal. by proxy 22 Feb. (HCA 7031/1 fo. 30). Preb. of Bartonsham 1526. Also preb. of Piona Parva. Biog. ref.: *BRUO 1500–40* p. 601.

M. Hugh Pole MA 1526–9

Coll. 6 Sept. 1526 (*Reg. Booth* p. 339). Instal. 7 Sept. (HCA 7031/1 fo. 38r). D. 26 July × 1 Aug. 1529 (TNA, PROB 11/25; *Reg. Booth* p. 343). Also treas. and preb. of Gorwell and Overbury, Hinton, Moreton and Whaddon and Norton. Biog. ref.: *BRUO* III 1490.

M. Geoffrey Downes DTh 1529–62

Coll. 1 Aug. 1529 (*Reg. Booth* p. 343). Instal. by proxy 5 Aug. (HCA 7031/1 fo. 61r). Occ. 1535 (*Valor* III 11), 28 June 1559 (*Reg. Parker* I 60) and 2 Jan. 1561 (HCA 7031/1 fo. 201v). D. by 20 July 1562 (York Minster Library, Acta Capitularia 1559–1673 fo. 11v). Biog. ref.: *BRUC* p. 193.

PREBENDARIES OF MORETON MAGNA

The endowment of this preb. was the rectory of Moreton on Lugg, Herefs., which was valued at £20 in 1291, 20m in 1294 and £19 14s 4d in 1535 (*Survey of Cath.* I 584; *Taxatio* p. 169b; *Reg. Swinfield* p. 305; *Valor* III 9).

Philip de Comite of Milan ?1291–?
Edward de Monte Martini 1307–?

Philip de Comite occ. *c.*1291 (*Taxatio* p. 169). Bp.'s mand. adm. Edward de Monte Martini 5 June 1307 by virtue of prov.; ineffective? (*Reg. Swinfield* p. 440). Philip occ. this preb. 12 June 1308 and res. a preb. of Hereford, probably this one, 19 Aug. 1311 when faculty gr. to card. Columpna to confer it on a fit person named by Andrew de Orto of Milan (HCA 7031/1 fo. 200; *CPL* II 87).

Anthony de Comite ?–1319

Gr. in 1311? (*CPL* II 87). Occ. as can. 8 Apr. 1318 (*Lettres Jean XXII* no. 6893). D. as preb. by 28 March 1319 (*CPR 1317–21* p. 321).

Adam de Herewynton 1319–44
M. John of Ross DCL ?–1325
John de Denton 1325

Royal gr. to Herewynton 28 March 1319 (*CPR 1317–21* p. 321) who occ. as can. 1 Jan. × 24 March 1320 (HCA R408). Ross held it sometime before becoming bp. of Carlisle, 1325 (*CPR 1324–7* p. 151) but this may be a scribal error for preb. of Moreton Parva. Royal gr. to Denton 17 Apr. 1325 (*ibid.* p. 116; *Reg. Orleton* p. 326). A dispute with bp. Orleton ensued (*CPR 1324–7* pp. 132, 151; *Reg. Orleton* pp. 326–8). Herewynton retained possession, though was absent from Hereford 24 June × 28 Sept. 1324 and 25 March × 23 June 1325 (HCA R412–13). Occ. as can. regularly from 24 June × 28 Sept. 1325 until 1 Jan. × 24 March 1338 (HCA R413–23). D. as preb. 31 March 1344 (Worcester, *Reg. Bransford* p. 379). Ross also archdcn. of Shropshire. Biog. ref.: Ross, *BRUO* III 1590–1; R. K. Rose, 'Ross, John (d. 1332)', *ODNB* <http://www.oxforddnb.com/view/article/24075>; Herewynton, M. Hodgetts, 'Adam of Herewynton', *Transactions of the Worcestershire Archaeological Society*, xxxvi (1959) pp. 33–41.

M. Thomas de Staunton BCL 1344–9
William de Kirkeby 1344

Expect. to Staunton 30 July 1342, still expect. 23 Jan. 1344 (*CPP* pp. 3, 38). Staunton occ. as can., probably this preb., 25 March × 23 June 1344 (HCA R429). Royal gr. to Kirkeby 20 March 1344 and 27 April (*CPR 1343–5* pp. 225, 241).

Staunton d. as preb. by 5 July 1349 (*CPP* p. 169). Biog. ref.: Staunton, *Hemingby's Register* pp. 232–3; *BRUC* p. 552.

M. Simon of Sudbury DCL 1349–61

Prov. 5 July 1349 (*CPP* p. 169). Estate ratif. 6 Feb. 1352 (*CPR 1350–4* p. 217). Bp. of London 1361, prov. 22 Oct., cons. 20 March 1362 (J. Le Neve, *Fasti Ecclesiae Anglicanae 1300–1541*, v: *St Paul's*, comp. J. M. Horn (1963) p. 2). Biog. ref.: *BRUO* III 2218; S. Walker, 'Sudbury, Simon (*c.*1316–81)', *ODNB* <http://www.oxforddnb.com/view/article/26759>.

Thomas Thebaud of Sudbury 1361–2
John Godewyk 1361
John Bishopston 1362–84

Prov. to Thomas Sudbury 11 Dec. 1361 on elevation of Simon of Sudbury to see of London, although illegitimate and under age without dispensation (*L&G* p. 195). Prov. to Godewyk 19 Oct. 1361 (*L&G* p. 247). Thomas Sudbury renounced right and royal gr. made to Bishopston 26 March 1362 (*CPR 1361–4* p. 180). Bp.'s mand. adm. 1 July 1363 (HCA 2252). Godewyk's rights reaffirmed by pope 19 Oct. but prov. not effective by 1366 × 1368 because Bishopston held preb. '*iure regio*' (*CPP* pp. 463–4; *L&G* p. 304). Still disputed in 1366 (Cant., *Reg. Langham* p. 105; London, *Reg. Sudbury* II 173). Bishopston occ. as can. 25 March × 23 June 1380 (HCA R445) and probably until d. by 11 Dec. 1384 (TNA, PROB11/1). Biog. ref.: Thebaud, *BRUO* III 2219; Godewyk, *BRUC* pp. 261–2.

M. John Prophete 1384–1407

Expect. 30 Oct. 1371 (*L&G* p. 447; *Lettres Gregoire XI* no. 8708). Royal gr. 8 Dec. 1384 (*CPR 1381–5* p. 490). Occ. 24 June × 28 Sept. 1385 (HCA R449). Second royal gr. 15 July 1389 (*CPR 1388–92* p. 87). Estate ratif. 15 May 1395 (*CPR 1391–6* p. 569). Exch. 8 Nov. 1407 with Thomas Felde for preb. Warham (*Reg. Mascall* p. 183). Also dean and preb. of Piona Parva. Biog. ref.: *BRUO* III 1521–3; R. G. Davies, 'Prophete, John (*c.*1350–1416)', *ODNB* <http://www.oxforddnb.com/view/article/37868>.

M. Thomas Felde DCL 1407–16

By exch. Nov. 1407. Res. by 23 Apr. 1416 (*Reg. Mascall* p. 181). Also dean and preb. of Warham and Withington Parva. Biog. ref.: *BRUO* II 682–3.

M. Thomas Walton BCL 1416–38

Coll. 23 Apr. 1416 (*Reg. Mascall* p. 181). Exch. 21 Jan 1438 with Maurice Winter for ch. of Cottenham, Cambs. (*Reg. Spofford* p. 369). Biog. ref.: *BRUC* p. 615.

M. Maurice Winter BCnL 1438–43

By exch. Jan 1438. Res. 31 May 1443 (*Reg. Spofford* p. 254). Biog. ref.: *BRUO* III 2126.

M. Richard Hoore BCn&CL 1443–50

Coll. 31 May 1443 (*Reg. Spofford* p. 365). D. by 30 Jan 1450 (*Reg. Beauchamp* p. 15). Biog. ref.: *BRUO* II 962.

M. Thomas Worshop or **Chesterfield** BCnL 1450–2

Coll. 30 Jan 1450 (*Reg. Beauchamp* p. 15). D. by Aug. 1452 (*ODNB*). Biog. ref.: *BRUO* III 2008; A. J. Kettle, 'Chesterfield, Thomas (d. 1452)', *ODNB* <http:// www.oxforddnb.com/view/article/5241>.

William Boulers 1452–?

Coll. 7 Sept. 1452 (*Reg. Boulers* p. 22). Occ. as can. 29 Sept. 1453 × 28 Sept. 1454 (HCA R491).

M. Richard Pede DCnL 1458–78

Coll. 25 Nov. 1458 (*Reg. Stanbury* p. 175). Exch. 25 July 1478 with Richard Martyn for preb. Huntington (*Reg. Myllyng* p. 202). Also dean, treas. and preb. of Hinton. Biog. ref.: *BRUO* III 1449–50.

M. Richard Martyn BCnL 1478–83

By exch. July 1478. Dispensation to hold preb. after cons. as bp. of St Davids 26 Apr. 1482 (*CPL* XIII ii 749). D. 11 May 1483 (*ODNB*). Also archdcn. of Hereford and preb. of Huntington, Pratum Minus and Putson Minor. Biog. ref.: *BRUO* II 1236–7; J. Hughes, 'Martyn, Richard (d. 1483)', *ODNB* <http://www.oxforddnb. com/view/article/18236>.

M. John Foster ?–1512

Occ. in Mayew's episcopate (1504–16) (*Reg. Mayew* p. 234). D. 18 Oct 1512 (*ibid.* p. 183). Biog. ref.: *BRUO* II 709–10.

M. William Webbe MA 1512–23

Coll. 22 Oct. 1512 (*Reg. Mayew* p. 280). Instal. 5 Nov. (HCA 7031/1 fo. 2r). D. 3 Nov. 1522 × 29 Jan. 1523 (HCA 7031/1 fo. 32v; *Reg. Booth* p. 335). Also archdcn. of Hereford and Shropshire and preb. of Gorwell and Overbury, Inkberrow and Wellington. Biog. ref.: *BRUO* III 2004.

M. Humphrey Ogle BCnL 1523–37

Coll. 29 Jan. 1523 (*Reg. Booth* p. 335). Res. by 23 July 1537 (*ibid.* p. 378). Also archdcn. of Shropshire and preb. of Eigne. Biog. ref.: *BRUO 1500–40* p. 423.

Thomas Soulement 1537–41

Coll. 23 July 1537 (*Reg. Booth* p. 378). Instal. by proxy 8 Aug. (HCA 7031/1 fo. 79v). D. 12 July 1541 (*ODNB*). Biog. ref.: P. R. N. Carter, 'Soulement, Thomas (b. in or before 1500, d. 1541)', *ODNB* <http://www.oxforddnb.com/view/ article/26043>.

M. Richard Thurkettil MA 1541–61

Coll. 26 July 1541 (HRO, AL 19/14 fo. 31r). Instal. 2 Sept. (HCA 7031/1 fo. 86r). Occ. 28 June 1559 (*Reg. Parker* I 60) and 2 Jan. 1561 (HCA 7031/1 fo. 201v); preb. vac. by 17 Apr. 1561 (HRO, AL 19/15 (Scory) fo. 4r).

PREBENDARIES OF MORETON PARVA

The endowment of this preb. was two carucates of land and rents in the parish of Moreton on Lugg, Herefs., which was valued at £10 in 1291, 10m in 1294 and £7 1s ½d in 1535 (*Survey of Cath.* I 586; *Taxatio* p. 169; *Reg. Swinfield* p. 305; *Valor* III 9).

Walter of Redmarley 1279–1302
Occ. as can. 1274 (BL, Harley Charter 54.H.53). Coll. 25 Dec. 1279 (*Reg. Cantilupe* p. 268). D. by 27 Sept. 1302 (*Reg. Swinfield* p. 534).

John of Kempsey 1302–3
Coll. 27 Sept. 1302 (*Reg. Swinfield* p. 534). Preb. of Colwall 1303. Also treas.

William de Caple 1303–10
Coll. 9 Nov. 1303 (*Reg. Swinfield* p. 535). D. by 24 Nov. 1310 (*ibid.* p. 540).

M. John of Ross DCL 1310–?
Coll. 24 Nov. 1310 (*Reg. Swinfield* p. 540). Bp. Carlisle 1325 (see preb. Moreton Magna). Also archdcn. of Shropshire. Biog. ref.: *BRUO* III 1590–1; R. K. Rose, 'Ross, John (d. 1332)', *ODNB* <http://www.oxforddnb.com/view/article/24075>.

M. John Orleton 1326–7
Coll. 16 Nov. 1326 (*Reg. Orleton* p. 389). Held *in commendam* for about a year (*ibid.* p. 389). Also preb. of Nonnington. Biog. ref.: *BRUO* II 1404.

Thomas Trillek 1327–63
William Huntlowe 1361
Coll. to Trillek 26 Sept. 1327 on a papal reservn. (*Reg. Orleton* p. 389). Estate ratif. 7 March 1328 (*CPR 1327–30* p. 250). Dean March 1355 (*Reg. Trillek* p. 388) but retained all ecclesiastical benefices (HCA 3161). Seems to have resigned deanery 1361 and royal gr. of this preb. to Huntlowe 23 July 1361 (*CPR 1361–4* p. 46). Huntlowe became preb. Inkberrow Nov. 1361 and Trillek still claimed preb. 23 Jan. 1363 (*CPP* p. 398). Preb. vac. 25 Nov. by his promotion to see of Chichester (*ibid.* p. 470). Huntlowe also claimed preb. of Huntington. Biog. ref.: Trillek, *BRUO* III 1906–8; D. Lepine, 'Trillek, Thomas (b. in or before 1312, d. 1372)', *ODNB* <http://www.oxforddnb.com/view/article/95196>.

M. Nicholas de Chaddesden DCL 1363
William de Gyddyng or Belles or Bello SchCn&CL ?1366–8
Prov. to Chaddesden 25 Nov. 1363 (*CPP* p. 470) but had not gained possession by 14 Oct. 1366 (Cant., *Reg. Langham* p. 57). Chaddesdon's prov. said to be ineffective 1366 × 1368 (*L&G* p. 286). Prov. to Gyddyng 26 Nov. 1363, still expect. 3 March 1364, in possession 17 Oct. 1366 (*CPP* p. 482; *L&G* p. 260; London, *Reg. Sudbury* II 173). Biog. ref.: Chaddesden, *BRUO* I 380–1.

M. Thomas Bushbury 1368–83?
M. William de Humberston 1369–72
John Ploufeld 1372–85

Coll. to Bushbury 8 March 1368 (*Reg. L. Charlton* p. 68); royal gr. 19 Jan. 1370 (*CPR 1367–70* p. 332). Prov. to Humberston 21 Nov. 1369 (*L&G* p. 403) and estate ratif. 26 Aug. 1372 (*CPR 1370–4* p. 187). Humberston exch. 4 Dec. 1372 with Ploufeld for preb. in St Martin's-le-Grand, London and in 1375 exch. another benefice for preb. of Ewithington (*Reg. Courtenay* p. 13). Bushbury's right affirmed by k. 12 Nov. 1377 (*CCR 1377–81* p. 26) and he occ. as can., probably this preb., 29 Sept. × 31 Dec. 1377 to 29 Sept. × 31 Dec. 1378 and 24 June × 28 Sept. 1383 (HCA R444, 444a, 447). Ploufeld may have gained possession by 22 July 1385 (*CPR 1385–9* p. 13). Bushbury preb. of Cublington 1403.

Thomas More 1385–6
M. John Godmanston 1385

Royal gr. to More of preb. held by John Ploufeld 22 July 1385 (*CPR 1385–9* p. 13; *Reg. Gilbert* p. 119). Royal gr. to Godmanston 19 Nov., revoked 21 Nov. (*CPR 1385–9* p. 70) but he occ. as can. 24 June × 28 Sept. 1385 (HCA R449). Coll. to More 30 July 1386 (*Reg. Gilbert* p. 119; *CPR 1385–9* pp. 384, 386). More preb. of Huntington by Jan. 1396. Godmanston also preb. of Norton, Putson Major and Withington Parva. Biog. ref.: More, Cant., *Reg Chichele* II 665.

M. John Kington BCn&CL 1402–10

Coll. 3 Nov. 1402 (*Reg. Trefnant* p. 185). Res. by 11 Feb. 1410 (*Reg. Mascall* p. 175). Biog. ref.: *BRUO* II 1075–6.

M. John Catterick LicCL 1410

Coll. 11 Feb. 1410 (*Reg. Mascall* p. 175). Res. 28 Feb. (*ibid.*). Biog. ref.: *BRUO* I 371–2.

Henry Bowet 1410–14

Coll. 4 March 1410 (*Reg. Mascall* p. 175). Res. by 23 May 1414 (*ibid.* p. 179). Biog. ref.: McDermid, *Beverley Fasti* pp. 53–4.

M. Nicholas Mockyng BCL 1414–24

Coll. 23 May 1414 (*Reg. Mascall* p. 179). D. 4 April × 10 June 1424 (TNA, PROB 11/3). Biog. ref.: *BRUC* pp. 407–8.

Henry Newton 1424–9

Coll. 2 July 1424 (*Reg. Spofford* p. 352). Preb. of Preston 1429.

M. John Asheby 1429–34

Coll. 28 Jan. 1429 (*Reg. Spofford* p. 355). Preb. of Cublington 1434. Also chanc. and treas.

M. William Walesby 1434–?

Coll. 9 Aug. 1434 (*Reg. Spofford* p. 359). Occ. 3 Sept. 1434 (HCA 2806).

M. John Langton BCnL ?–1441

Occ. 28 Dec. 1438 (*CPL* IX 36) Exch. 30 June 1441 with William Walesby for ch. of St Peter de Langton, Linc. dioc. (*Reg. Spofford* p. 369). Also preb. of Huntington. Biog. ref.: *BRUC* pp. 351–2.

M. William Walesby 1441–?

By exch. June 1441.

M. Thomas Bolyen ?–1446

Occ. as can. 29 Sept. 1444 × 28 Sept. 1445 (HCA R483). Exch. this preb. 16 May 1446 with William Saunders for preb. in St Stephen's Westminster (*CPR 1441–6* p. 438). Exch. effected 8 Jan. 1447 (*Reg. Spofford* p. 367). Biog. ref.: *BRUC* pp. 70–1.

M. William Saunders 1446–?

By exch. May 1446. Occ. 14 June 1462 (*Reg. Stanbury* p. 75).

M. David Husband DCnL ?–1469

Res. this preb. by 25 May 1469 (*Reg. Stanbury* p. 186). Biog. ref.: *BRUO* II 989.

M. William Gifford DTh 1469–72

Coll. 25 May 1469 (*Reg. Stanbury* p. 186). Res. by 11 Nov. 1472 (*ibid.* p. 188). Biog. ref.: *BRUO* II 763–4.

M. William Wrixham DTh 1472–82

Coll. 11 Nov. 1472 (*Reg. Stanbury* p. 188). Res. 20 Aug. 1482 (*Reg. Myllyng* p. 193). Biog. ref.: *BRUO* III 2095.

M. William FitzHerbert DCnL 1482–?

Coll. 20 Aug. 1482 (*Reg. Myllyng* p. 193). Biog. ref.: *BRUO* II 689.

M. Miles Ragon ?–1512

Occ. as can. 29 Sept. 1503 × 28 Sept. 1504 (HCA R544). Res. this preb. by 25 Oct. 1512 to become preb. Preston (*Reg. Mayew* p. 280).

M. Nicholas Walwen 1512–44/5

Coll. 25 Oct. 1512 (*Reg. Mayew* p. 280). Instal. 27 Nov. (HCA 7031/1 fo. 2r). D. 15 Dec. 1544 × 23 May 1545 (HCA 7031/1 fo. 91v; HRO, AL 19/14 fo. 61v). Also treas. and preb. of Eigne. Biog. ref.: *BRUO 1500–40* p. 707.

PREBENDARIES OF NONNINGTON

The endowment of this preb. was land at Nonnington in the parish of Withington, Herefs., which was valued at £12 14s in 1291, 12m in 1294 and £11 13s 4d in 1535 (*Survey of Cath.* I 588; *Taxatio* p. 169a; *Reg. Swinfield* p. 305; *Valor* III 10).

M. William de Gaye or **de la Gare** 1295–1304
Coll. 25 July 1295 (*Reg. Swinfield* p. 530). D. by 24 March 1304 (*ibid.* p. 535). Also treas.

M. Richard de Dunre 1304–22
Coll. 24 March 1304 (*Reg. Swinfield* p. 535). D. by 15 July 1322 (*Reg. Orleton* p. 388n.). Biog. ref.: *BRUO* I 607.

M. John Orleton 1322–41
Coll. 15 July 1322 (*Reg. Orleton* p. 388); also held preb. Moreton Parva *in commendam* for about a year 1326–7 (*ibid.* p. 389). Last occ. 24 June × 28 Sept. 1341 (HCA R426) probably this preb. Biog. ref.: *BRUO* II 1404.

M. Richard Chaundos 1341–98
Coll. 28 Aug. 1341 (*Reg. T. Charlton* p. 82). D. 17 Oct. 1398 (HCA R630).

John Hereford or **Carpenter** 1398–1427?
Coll. 18 Oct. 1398 (*Reg. Trefnant* p. 182). Estate ratif. 18 Dec. 1399 (*CPR 1399–1401* p. 136). Resident 29 Sept. 1424 × 28 Sept. 1425, last occ. 2 Apr. 1426 and res. canonical house by 1 March 1427 (HCA R153–4, 637; *Reg. Spofford* p. 353). Also archdcn. of Hereford and Shropshire.

M. Thomas Makeblith ?–1431
D. as preb. by 15 March 1431 (*Reg. Spofford* p. 357). Biog. ref.: *BRUO* II 1206.

Richard Martin 1431–3
Coll. 15 March 1431 (*Reg. Spofford* p. 357). Exch. 18 Dec. 1433 with John Home for ch. of South Molton, Devon (*ibid.* p. 369). Also preb. of Wellington.

John Home 1433–73
By exch. Dec. 1433. D. 26 Nov. 1473 (*Survey of Caths.* I 588; HCA R509).

David Hopton ?–1479
Occ. as can. 29 Sept. 1475 × 28 Sept. 1476 (HCA R512). Res. this preb. by 27 Oct. 1479 (*Reg. Myllyng* p. 190). Also preb. of Colwall.

M. Walter Oudeby DCnL 1479–85
Coll. 27 Oct. 1479 (*Reg. Myllyng* p. 190). Res. 15 Sept. 1485 (*ibid.* p. 194). Biog. ref.: *BRUC* pp. 473–8.

M. Richard Fox BCL 1485–7
Coll. 16 Sept. 1485 (*Reg. Myllyng* p. 194). Bp. of Exeter 1487. Biog. ref.: *BRUO* II 715–19; C. S. L. Davies, 'Fox, Richard (1447/8–1528)', *ODNB* <http://www.oxforddnb.com/view/article/10051>.

M. Polydore Vergil or **Castellensis** ?–1555

Occ. 1504 as 'factorem et negociorem gestorem reverendi [patri] Hadriani', though not certainly preb. (*Reg. Mayew* p. 42). Perhaps 'Came into it about 1507' (*Survey of Cath*. I 588), but that is pure supposition. Occ. holding this preb. on list of prebs. probably dating to *c*.1508 × July 1511 (HRO, AL 19/12 fo. 137r). Occ. as can. 29 Sept. 1517 × 28 Sept. 1518 (HCA, R558). D. at Urbino 18 Apr. 1555 (notarial attestation on will, printed in *Transactions of the Royal Historical Society*, 4th ser., xi (1928) p. 136). Biog. ref.: W. J. Connell, 'Vergil, Polydore (*c*.1470–1555)', *ODNB* <http://www.oxforddnb.com/view/article/28645>.

PREBENDARIES OF NORTON

The endowment of this preb. was land in the parish of Norton Canon, Herefs., valued at 9s ¼d in 1291 and £2 3s 2d in 1535 (*Survey of Cath*. I 590; *Taxatio* p. 169a; *Valor* III 11).

John of Scarborough ?–1305

Occ. as can. 6 Apr. 1286 and 1289 (*Reg. Swinfield* p. 549; *Les Registres de Nicolas IV*, ed. E. Langlois (Bibliothèque des Ecoles Françaises d'Athènes et de Rome, 2nd ser., v, Paris, 1886–1905) no. 1624). D. as preb. by 6 March 1305 (*Reg. Swinfield* p. 536).

M. Richard de Bello or **de la Battayle** 1305–26

Coll. 6 March 1305 (*Reg. Swinfield* p. 536). D. by 8 Sept. 1326 (*Reg. Orleton* p. 389). Biog. ref.: *BRUO* I 556.

Thomas of Evesham 1326
Roger Braynton 1326–49

Royal gr. 7 Sept. 1326 to Evesham (*CPR 1324–7* p. 319). Coll. 8 Sept. to Braynton (*Reg. Orleton* p. 389) who was regularly resident from 29 Sept. × 31 Dec. 1327 to 29 Sept. 1347 × 28 Sept. 1348 (HCA R414–31, 136). Papal mand. 19 June 1343 for prov. to larger preb. of Hereford in place of his small one (*CPL* III 99). Preb. of Hunderton 1349. Also preb. of Wellington.

John Prophete 1349–60/1
M. William de Herewynton DCL 1350

Prophete conf. as successor to Reginald Brynton [*sic*], 1 Aug. 1349 × 7 Apr. 1350 (*L&G* pp. 78, 110). Conf. accepted by Prophete 9 Sept. 1350 and he occ. regularly until 29 Sept. 1360 × 28 Sept. 1361 (*CPP* p. 205; HCA R142). Prov. to Herewynton 7 Apr. 1350 but ineffective (*L&G* p. 110; *CPP* p. 195). Prophete also preb. of Warham.

Thomas Shifford 1361–71

Expect. 24 Jan. 1355 (*CPL* III 543). Occ. as can. 1 Jan. × 24 March 1361 (HCA R438). Exch. 5 March 1371 with Thomas Stayndrop for ch. of Wappenbury, Warwicks. (*Reg. Courtenay* p. 13).

Thomas Stayndrop 1371–6

By exch. March 1371. Exch. this preb. and ch. of North Tawton, Devon 8 Nov. 1376 with Robert Vaggescombe for ch. of Parkham, Devon (Exeter, *Reg. Brantingham* p. 47).

Robert Vaggescombe 1376–82?

By exch. Nov. 1376. Occ. as can. 25 March × 23 June 1378 (HCA R444). D. 30 April × 16 June 1382, as preb.? (Exeter, *Reg. Brantingham* pp. 77, 465).

M. John Godmanston ?1382–3

Expect. 15 May 1378 (HCA 2844); notorial instrument recording this 18 May 1381 (*ibid.*). Exch. this preb. 8 July 1383 with John Harold for free chap. of Reynalton, Pemb. (*Reg. Gilbert* p. 123). Also preb. of Moreton Parva, Putson Major and Withington Parva.

M. John Harold BCn&CL 1383–90

By exch. July 1383. Preb. of Bullinghope 1390. Also dean and preb. of Moreton and Whaddon. Biog. ref.: *BRUO* III 877.

Simon Burley 1390

Occ. as can. unidentified preb. 1380–7. D. as preb. 18 × 25 Sept. 1390 (HCA 2822; *Reg. Trefnant* p. 174).

Reginald Wolstone 1390–6
M. Thomas Leche BCL 1393
Thomas Wybbe or **Webbe** 1394

Coll. to Wolstone 25 Sept. 1390 (*Reg. Trefnant* p. 174). Expect. to Leche 'recently' by 1 May 1392 and prov. to this preb. 12 May 1393 but ineffective (*CPL* IV 392, 467). Wybbe had prov. before 1 May 1398 and occ. as can. 24 June × 28 Sept. 1394 but unable to retain it (HCA R456; *CPL* V 165). Wolstone occ. as can. from 29 Sept. × 31 Dec. 1390 to 24 June × 28 Sept 1396 (HCA R454–8). He became preb. of Hinton 1396.

William Peion or **Pigeon** *alias* **Berowne** 1396–1417/18?
Thomas Wybbe or **Webbe** 1398

Coll. to Peion 1 Oct. 1396 (*Reg. Trefnant* p. 181). Wybbe gr. expect. despite ineffective earlier prov. 1 May 1398 (*CPL* V 165). Peion last occ. as can. 29 Sept. 1417 × 28 Sept. 1418 (HCA R151).

John Burrell 1416?–36
Richard Kingston 1418

Royal gr. to Burrell 23 Jan. 1416 (*CPR 1416–22* p. 59) but Peion not d. and continues in a/c rolls until 1417–18 (HCA R151). Burrell had gained possession by 16 Aug. 1418 when coll. to Kingston on alleged d. of Burrell (HCA 2787). Burrell not d., occ. this preb. 29 Sept. 1418 × 28 Sept. 1419 and res. by 25 Aug. 1436 (HCA R636; *Reg. Spofford* p. 361). Kingston also archdcn. of Hereford and preb. of Bullinghope and Cublington. Biog. ref.: Kingston, McDermid, *Beverley Fasti* pp. 64–5.

M. Simon Alcock DTh 1436–59
Coll. 25 Aug. 1436 (*Reg. Spofford* p. 361). D. 10 Aug 1459 m.i. Lincoln cath. (*Reg. Stanbury* p. 176; *Survey of Caths.* I 590). Biog. ref.: *BRUO* I 18–19.

Richard Homme 1459–66
Coll. 24 Aug. 1459 (*Reg. Stanbury* p. 176). D. by 2 Oct. 1466 (*ibid.* p. 183).

Richard Hyde 1466–7
Coll. 2 Oct. 1466 (*Reg. Stanbury* p. 183). D. by 1 Nov. 1467 (*ibid.* p. 185).

M. William Bagart BCL 1467–?
Coll. 1 Nov. 1467 (*Reg. Stanbury* p. 185). Occ. this preb. 29 Sept. 1467 × 28 Sept. 1468 (HCA R637c). Biog. ref.: *BRUO* I 90.

Richard Burton ?–1504
One M. Burton occ. as can. 1492–3 (HCA R530). D. as preb. by 31 Oct. 1504 (*Reg. Mayew* p. 273).

M. Henry Martin BCn&CL 1504–8
Coll. 31 Oct 1504 (*Reg. Mayew* p. 273). Preb. of Warham 1508. Also archdcn. of Hereford and Shropshire and preb. of Gorwell and Overbury, Inkberrow and Withington Parva. Biog. ref.: *BRUO* II 1234.

M. Edmund Froucetur DTh 1508–9
Coll. 19 Oct. 1508 (*Reg. Mayew* p. 276). Preb. of Putson Major 1509. Also dean, treas. and preb. of Colwall. Biog. ref.: *BRUO* II 732.

M. Hugh Pole MA 1510–11
Coll. 19 May 1510 (*Reg. Mayew* p. 278). Preb. of Hinton 1511. Also treas. and preb. of Gorwell and Overbury and Moreton and Whaddon. Biog. ref.: *BRUO* III 1490.

John Oliver or **Smythe** 1511–12
Coll. 25 July 1511 (*Reg. Mayew* p. 278). Preb. of Hinton 1512. Biog. ref.: *BRUO 1500–40* p. 425.

M. Thomas Chipnam MA 1512–16
Coll. 16 July 1512 (*Reg. Mayew* p. 280). Instal. s.d. (HCA 7031/1 fo. 1r). Res. by 7 Apr. 1516 (*Reg. Mayew* p. 284). Biog. ref.: *BRUO* I 418.

M. Richard Parkhurst MA 1516–29
Coll. 7 Apr. 1516 (*Reg. Mayew* p. 284). Res. by 21 Nov. 1529 (*Reg. Booth* p. 343). Biog. ref.: *BRUO* III 1428–9.

M. William Marbule BCL 1529–53
Coll. 21 Nov. 1529 (*Reg. Booth* p. 343). Instal. 4 Dec. (HCA 7031/1 fo. 64r). D. by 11 Oct. 1552 (HCA 7031/1 fo. 113r). Biog. ref.: *BRUO* II 1219–20.

PREBENDARIES OF PIONA PARVA

The endowment of this preb. was land in the parish of Canons Pyon, Herefs., which was valued at £1 in 1291 and 1294, and £1 16s 4d in 1535 (*Survey of Cath.* I 593; *Taxatio* p. 169a; *Reg. Swinfield* p. 305; *Valor* III 12).

M. Thomas of Cobham DCnL 1299–1317
Coll. 5 Dec. 1299 (*Reg. Swinfield* p. 531). Bp. of Worcester 1317, prov. 31 March, cons. 22 May (J. Le Neve, *Fasti Ecclesiae Anglicanae 1300–1541*, iv: *Monastic Cathedrals*, comp. B. Jones (1963) p. 55). Biog. ref.: R. M. Haines, 'Cobham, Thomas (*c.*1265–1327)', *ODNB* <http://www.oxforddnb.com/view/article/5745>; *BRUO* I 450–1.

Roger Northburgh 1317–18
M. Roger Nassington 1317
Royal gr. to Northburgh 20 Apr. 1317, to Nassington 29 May (*CPR 1313–17* pp. 639, 655). Second royal gr. to Northburgh 15 June of the preb. 'which Roger Nassington lately held' (*ibid.* p. 658). Northburgh exch. 6 Jan. 1318 with Nicholas Hugate for preb. of Yatesbury in Salisbury (*Reg. Orleton* pp. 55–6; *The Registers of Roger Martival, Bishop of Salisbury, 1315–30*, ed. K. Edwards *et al.* (4 vols., Canterbury and York Soc., lv, lvii–ix, lxviii, 1959–75) I 100). Biog. ref.: Northburgh, R. M. Haines, 'Northburgh, Roger (d. 1358)', *ODNB* <http://www.oxforddnb.com/view/article/20325>; Nassington, *BRUO* II 1338.

Nicholas Hugate 1318–?
By exch. Jan. 1318. Bp.'s mand. adm. 12 Jan. (*Reg. Orleton* p. 56). D. 24 June 1338, as preb.? (*Memorials of Beverley Minster: the Chapter Act Book of the Collegiate Church of St John of Beverley, AD 1286–1347*, ed. A. F. Leach (2 vols., Surtees Soc., xcviii, cviii, 1898–1903) II 120). Biog. ref.: McDermid, *Beverley Fasti* pp. 36–7.

John de Sheynton 1341–5
Coll. 4 June 1341 (*Reg. T. Charlton* p. 82). Exch. by 6 June 1345 with Griffin Charlton for portion in Pontesbury colleg. ch., Salop. (*Reg. Trillek* p. 28).

M. Griffin Charlton 1345–85
By exch. June 1345. Coll. 22 Oct. (*Reg. Trillek* p. 373). D. 21 Jan. × 25 Feb. 1385 (*Reg. Gilbert* pp. 66, 118). Also preb. of Bullinghope. Biog. ref.: *BRUO* I 390.

M. Roger Hore 1385–1407
Occ. as can. 24 June × 28 Sept. 1385 (HCA R449). Estate ratif. 21 Aug. 1389 (*CPR 1388–92* p. 108). Exch. 16 Nov. 1407 with John Prophete for preb. of Warham (*Reg. Mascall* p. 183).

M. John Prophete 1407–8
By exch. Nov. 1407. Res. by 22 Sept. 1408 (*Reg. Mascall* p. 174). Also dean and preb. of Moreton, Magna and Warham. Biog. ref.: *BRUO* III 1521–3; R. G.

Davies, 'Prophete, John (*c*.1350–1416)', *ODNB* <http://www.oxforddnb.com/view/article/37868>.

M. John Bosham 1408–44

Coll. 22 Sept. 1408 (*Reg. Mascall* p. 174). Last occ. as can. 29 Sept. 1443 × 28 Sept. 1444 (HCA R483). Biog. ref.: *BRUO* I 255.

M. Richard Chester DTh 1444–9

Occ. as can. 29 Sept. 1444 × 28 Sept. 1445 (HCA R483). Exch. this preb. 5 March 1449 with Elias Holcote for preb. of Twiford in St Paul's, London (*Reg. Beauchamp* p. 15). Biog. ref.: *BRUO* I 407–8.

M. Elias Holcote BTh 1449–51

By exch. March 1449. Res. by 30 July 1451 (*Reg. Boulers* p. 22). Biog. ref.: *BRUO* II 945–6.

M. John Sutton MA 1451–?

Coll. 30 July 1451 (*Reg. Boulers* p. 22). Occ. 14 June 1462 (*Reg. Stanbury* p. 75) and one M. Sutton occ. as can. 29 Sept. 1472 × 28 Sept. 1473 (HCA R509). D., as preb.?, by 8 March 1480 (J. Le Neve, *Fasti Ecclesiae Anglicanae 1300–1541*, v: *St Paul's*, comp. J. M. Horn (1963) p. 60). Biog. ref.: *BRUO* III 1821.

M. Ralph Hauyes BCnL 1486–8

Coll. 19 Nov. 1486 (*Reg. Myllyng* p. 195). Preb. of Eigne 1488. Also preb. of Wellington.

M. David William DCnL ?1488–92?

Occ. as preb. 1486 × 1493 (TNA, C 1/111/74); probably in succession to Hauyes and until d. 28 Sept. 1491 × 1492 (TNA, PROB 11/9; *BRUO* III 2049–50). Biog. ref.: *BRUO* III 2049–50.

M. Benedict Dodyne ?1492/3–1504

One M. Benedict occ. as can. 29 Sept. 1492 × 28 Sept. 1493 (HCA R530). Dodyne occ. as can. 3 Oct 1497 (*CPL* XVII i 8). Res. this preb. April/May 1504 (*Reg. Mayew* pp. 43–6). Biog. ref.: *BRUC* pp. 189–90.

M. Hugh Grene 1504–11

Coll. after Apr./May 1504 (*Reg. Mayew* pp. 43, 46) and occ. as can. 29 Sept. 1503 × 28 Sept. 1504 (HCA R544). Charged with simony 1508 (*Reg. Mayew* pp. 35–47). Preb. of Pratum Majus 1511.

M. William Delabere 1511–12

Coll. 17 July 1511 (*Reg. Mayew* p. 278). Preb. of Eigne 1512. Also preb. of Pratum Majus.

John Viall 1512–13

Coll. 11 Dec. 1512 (*Reg. Mayew* p. 280). Instal. 18 Dec. (HCA 7031/1 fo. 2r). Preb. of Putson Minor 1513. Biog. ref.: *BRUO 1500–40* p. 707.

M. Jon Kidwelly BCn&CL 1513–14
Coll. 15 Aug. 1513 (*Reg. Mayew* p. 281). D. by 8 Feb. 1514 (*ibid.*). Biog. ref.: *BRUO* II 1066.

M. William Goberd BA 1514–15
Coll. 8 Feb. 1514 (*Reg. Mayew* p. 281). D. 18 Dec. 1515 (*BRUO 1500–40* p. 236). Also treas., archdcn. of Shropshire and preb. of Moreton and Whaddon. Biog. ref.: *BRUO 1500–40* p. 236.

M. David Walker BCL 1516–22
Coll. 3 Jan. 1516 (*Reg. Mayew* p. 284). Instal. Jan. (HCA 7031/1 fo. 7v). Preb. of Moreton and Whaddon 1522. Also preb. of Bartonsham. Biog. ref.: *BRUO 1500–40* p. 601.

M. William Burghill DCnL 1522–3
Coll. 1 March 1522 (*Reg. Booth* p. 334). Instal. 17 Apr. (HCA 7031/1 fo. 30v). Exch. 27 Nov. 1523 with George Mason for preb. of Bartonsham (*Reg. Booth* p. 336). Also treas. Biog. ref.: *BRUO 1500–40* p. 85.

M. George Mason BA 1523–4
By exch. Nov. 1523. Instal. 30 Nov. (HCA 7031/1 fo. 33). Preb. of Church Withington 1524. Also preb. of Bartonsham. Biog. ref.: *BRUO 1500–40* p. 386.

M. John Herring BCnL 1524–33
Coll. 1 May 1524 (*Reg. Booth* p. 337). Instal. 23 Nov. (HCA 7031/1 fo. 36r). Res. by 28 Feb. 1533 (*Reg. Booth* p. 347). Biog. ref.: *BRUO* II 919.

M. Robert Bygge BTh 1533–8/9
Coll. 28 Feb. 1533 (*Reg. Booth* p. 347). Instal. 4 March (HCA 7031/1 fo. 70v). D. by 7 Jan. 1539 (HCA 7031/1 fo. 83). Biog. ref.: *BRUO 1500–40* p. 92.

M. Robert Sparcheford MA 1539–59/60
Coll. 1 Apr. 1539 (*Reg. Booth* p. 384). Instal. s.d. (HCA 7031/1 fo. 79v). Occ. 28 June 1559 (*Reg. Parker* I 60); preb. vac. by 28 June 1560 by d. of last incumbent (?Sparcheford) (HRO, AL 19/15 (Scory) fo. 1v). Also archdcn. of Shropshire. Biog. ref.: *BRUO 1500–40* p. 530.

PREBENDARIES OF PRATUM MAJUS

The endowment of this preb. was a truss of hay from Lugg Meadow which formed part of the tithes belonging to the ch. of Marden. It was valued at 2d in 1291 and £2 1s 8½d in 1535 (*Survey of Cath.* I 595; *Taxatio* p. 169a; *Valor* III 11).

Alan de Crepping DCL ?–1300
Occ. as can. 9 Aug. 1272 (HCA 2868). Occ. this preb. 1291 (*Taxatio* p. 169). D. by 22 Aug. 1300 (*Reg. Swinfield* p. 547). Biog. ref.: *BRUO* I 512.

M. Philip Talbot 1300–9

Coll. 22 Aug. 1300 (*Reg. Swinfield* p. 532). Last occ. as can. 29 Sept. 1307 × 28 Sept. 1308 (HCA R124), probably until d. by 15 × 25 July 1309 (*Reg. Swinfield* pp. 449–51). Also archdcn. of Shropshire.

M. Richard Sydenhale ?1339–48

Occ. as can. 1 Jan. × 24 March 1339 (HCA R424), probably this preb. Exch. this preb. and treasurership by 2 Dec. 1348 with John Boter for ch. of Staunton-on-Wye, Herefs. (*Reg. Trillek* pp. 40, 406). Also archdcn. of Shropshire.

John Boter 1348–78?

By exch. Dec. 1348. Last occ. as can. 1 Jan. × 24 March 1378 (HCA R444). Also treas.

M. John Abraham ?1383–94

First occ. as can. 25 March × 23 June 1383 (HCA R447). D. as preb. by 21 June 1394 (*Reg. Trefnant* p. 178).

M. Nicholas Hereford DTh 1394–*c*.1416

Hereford had expect. to preb. and dig. 26 March 1371 (*L&G* p. 424) and succeeded to Abraham's unnamed preb. 21 June 1394 (*Reg. Trefnant* p. 178). He exch. it sometime before 1417 with John Sellow for preb. of Pratum Minus (*BRUO* II 1667). Also chanc., treas. and preb. of Putson Minor. Biog. ref.: *BRUO* II 1667.

M. John Sellow BCn&CL *c*.1416–33

By exch. *c*.1416. Res. this preb. by 7 Sept. 1433 (*Reg. Spofford* p. 359). Also preb. of Pratum Minus. Biog. ref.: *BRUO* III 1667–8.

William Beford or **Blower** 1433–48/9?

Coll. 7 Sept. 1433 (*Reg. Spofford* p. 359). Last occ. as can. 29 Sept. 1448 × 28 Sept. 1449 (HCA R486).

M. John Clone ?1458/9–60

First occ. as can. 29 Sept. 1458 × 28 Sept. 1459 (HCA R495). Res. this preb. by 15 March 1460 to become preb. of Hinton (*Reg. Stanbury* p. 176).

Hugh Ragon 1460–2

Coll. 15 March 1460 (*Reg. Stanbury* p. 176). Preb. Withington Parva 1462. Also preb. of Gorwell and Overbury and unidentified preb.

M. John Grenewey 1462–6

Coll. 14 Apr. 1462 (*Reg. Stanbury* p. 178). Preb. Warham 1466.

M. William Rawlyns BCnL 1466–7

Coll. 8 Apr. 1466 (*Reg. Stanbury* p. 182). D. by 24 Feb. 1467 (*ibid.* p. 184). Biog. ref.: *BRUO* III 1552.

M. Ralph Barton 1467–76

Coll. 24 Feb. 1467 (*Reg. Stanbury* p. 184). Res. this preb by 16 Nov. 1476 but held another unknown preb. from 1478/9 until 1492/3 (*Reg. Myllyng* p. 187; HCA R168–75). Biog. ref.: *BRUC* p. 42.

M. William Vauce BCn&CL 1476–9

Coll. 16 Nov. 1476 (*Reg. Myllyng* p. 187). D. by 30 July 1479 (*ibid.* p. 189). Biog. ref.: *BRUO* III 1943–4.

Richard Cornwaile 1479–?

Coll. 30 July 1479 (*Reg. Myllyng* p. 189).

M. Thomas Chaundler DTh ?1480/1–6

Occ. as can. 29 Sept. 1480 × 28 Sept. 1481 (HCA R517). Res. this preb. by 2 Jan. 1486 to become preb. of Gorewell and Overbury (*Reg. Myllyng* p. 194). Also dean. Biog. ref.: *BRUO* I 398–9; J. Catto, 'Chaundler, Thomas (*c*.1417–90)', *ODNB* <http://www.oxforddnb.com/view/article/5200>.

M. Alexander King 1486–7

Coll. 2 Jan 1486 (*Reg. Myllyng* p. 194). D. by 10 March 1487 (*CPR 1485–94* p. 154). Biog. ref.: *BRUC* pp. 342–3.

M. Roger Brayne BCnL ?1505/6–9

Occ. as can. 29 Sept. 1505 × 28 Sept. 1506 (HCA R545). Res. this preb. by 7 Feb. 1509 to become preb. of Warham (*Reg. Mayew* p. 276). Also treas. Biog. ref.: *BRUO* I 255–6.

M. William Delabere 1509–11

Coll. 7 Feb. 1509 (*Reg. Mayew* p. 276). Preb. of Piona Parva 1511. Also preb. of Eigne.

M. Hugh Grene 1511–24

Coll. 17 July 1511 (*Reg. Mayew* p. 278). D. by 27 Jan 1524 (*Reg. Booth* p. 336). Also preb. of Piona Parva.

M. John Cragge MA 1524–6

Coll. 27 Jan. 1524 (*Reg. Booth* p. 336). Instal. 26 [*sic*] Jan. (HCA 7031/1 fo. 33r). Preb. of Gorewell and Overbury 1526. Biog. ref.: *BRUO 1500–40* p. 148.

Richard Baldwin 1526–42

Coll. 6 Sept. 1526 (*Reg. Booth* p. 339). Instal. by proxy 7 Sept. (HCA 7031/1 fo. 38r). Res. by 19 June 1542 (HRO, AL 19/14 fo. 38v), and presumably by 9 June when William Barret accounted for first fruits on this preb. (TNA, E 334/2 fo. 105).

PREBENDARIES OF PRATUM MINUS

The endowment of this preb. was an acre of meadow in Lugg Meadow which formed part of the tithes belonging to the ch. of Marden, but was said to be half an acre in 1294. It was valued at 6d in 1291, 3d in 1294 and £1 19s ¼d in 1535 (*Survey of Cath.* I 596; *Taxatio* p. 169a; *Reg. Swinfield* p. 305; *Valor* III 11).

M. William of Kingscote DCnL 1293–1303
Coll. 21 March 1293 (*Reg. Swinfield* p. 529). Preb. of Preston 1303. Biog. ref.: *BRUO* II 1074.

M. James Berkeley MA 1303–27
Coll. 17 May 1303 (*Reg. Swinfield* p. 534). Bp. of Exeter 1327. Biog. ref.: *BRUO* I 174–5; N. I. Orme, 'Berkeley, James (*c.*1275–1327)', *ODNB* <http://www.oxforddnb.com/view/article/95144>.

M. William Fownhope 1327–56
Coll. 26 Sept. 1327 (*Reg. Orleton* p. 389). Estate ratif. 7 March 1328 (*CPR 1327–30* p. 250). D. by 1 Apr. 1356 (*Reg. Trillek* p. 389).

Baldwin Whitney 1356–69
Prov. to unnamed preb. 22 Apr. 1353, still expect. 22 June 1353 (*CPP* pp. 243, 248). Coll. 1 Apr. 1356 (*Reg. Trillek* p. 389). Papal conf. 26 May 1356 and 25 June 1359 (*L&G* p. 148; *CPP* pp. 312, 344). Occ. 18 Nov. 1366 (Cant., *Reg. Langham* p. 41), probably until d. by 3 Sept. 1369 (Lincolnshire Archives Office, Reg. X fo. 245v). Biog. ref.: A. H. Thompson, 'Pluralism in the medieval church; with notes on pluralists in the diocese of Lincoln, 1366', *Associated Architectural and Archaeological Reports and Papers*, xxxvi (1921–2) 24.

Walter Almaly 1369–89
Expect. 24 March 1366 (*CPP* p. 519). Royal gr. 22 Aug. 1369 (*CPR 1367–70* p. 300). D. by 12 Sept. 1389 (*CPR 1388–92* p. 103).

John Excestre 1389–96
Royal gr. 12 Sept. 1389 (*CPR 1388–92* p. 103). Exch. 18 Oct. 1396 with Walter Trote for preb. in colleg. ch. of St Chad, Lichfield (*Reg. Trefnant* p. 190).

Walter Trote 1396–1403
By exch. Oct. 1396. Res. by 11 June 1403 (*Reg. Trefnant* p. 186).

M. John Gorwell 1403–6
Coll. 11 June 1403 (*Reg. Trefnant* p. 186; *The Register of Edmund Stafford, Bishop of Exeter, 1395–1419: an Index and Abstract of its Contents*, ed. F. C. Hingeston-Randolph (1886) pp. 116, 177). Res. by 30. July 1406 (*Reg. Mascall* p. 169). Biog. ref.: *BRUO* II 792.

Thomas Shelford 1406–10
Coll. 30 July 1406 (*Reg. Mascall* p. 169). Res. by 19 March 1410 (*ibid.* p. 175).

M. John Sellow BCn&CL 1410–16
Coll. 19 March 1410 (*Reg. Mascall* p. 175). Exch. with Nicholas Hereford for preb. Pratum Majus *c.*1416 (*BRUO* III 1667). Biog. ref.: *BRUO* III 1667–8.

M. Nicholas Hereford DTh *c.*1416–17
By exch. *c.*1416. Res. this preb. 2 Nov. 1417 (*Reg. Lacy H* p. 113). Also chanc., treas. and preb. of Pratum Majus and Putson Minor. Biog. ref.: *BRUO* II 913–15.

William Bailly 1417–45/6?
Coll. 4 Nov. 1417 (*Reg. Lacy H* 113). Occ. as can. until 29 Sept. 1445 × 28 Sept. 1446 (HCA R484).

M. Thomas Yone BCnL ?1445/6–72
Occ. as can. from 29 Sept. 1445 × 28 Sept. 1446 (HCA R484). Occ. as preb. 14 June 1462 (*Reg. Stanbury* p. 75). Also chanc. and archdcn. of Shropshire. D. by 24 Nov. 1472 (*ibid.* p. 188). Biog. ref.: *BRUO* III 2134.

M. Richard Martyn BCnL 1472–4
Coll. 28 Nov. 1472 (*Reg. Stanbury* p. 188). Preb. of Putson Minor 1474. Also archdcn. of Hereford and preb. of Huntington and Moreton Magna. Biog. ref.: *BRUO* II 1236–7; J. Hughes, 'Martyn, Richard (d. 1483)', *ODNB* <http://www.oxforddnb.com/view/article/18236>.

M. Roger Griffith MA 1474–87
Coll. 10 March 1474 (*Reg. Stanbury* p. 189). D. by 12 Oct. 1487 (*Reg. Myllyng* p. 196). Biog. ref.: *BRUO* II 825–6.

M. Walter Hylle SchTh 1487–1494
Coll. 12 Oct. 1487 (*Reg. Myllyng* p. 196). D. 30 March 1494 (*BRUO* II 994). Biog. ref.: *BRUO* II 994.

M. Reginald West ?–1508
Res. this preb. by 5 July 1508 (*Reg. Mayew* p. 275). Also dean. Biog. ref.: *BRUO* III 2019.

M. Thomas Wolsey MA 1508–13
Coll. 5 July 1508 (*Reg. Mayew* p. 275). Res. 27 Jan. 1513 (*ibid.* p. 281; *Reg. Booth* p. 17). Also dean. Biog. ref.: *BRUO* III 2077–80; S. M. Jack, 'Wolsey, Thomas (1470/1–1530)', *ODNB* <http://www.oxforddnb.com/view/article/29854>.

M. William Edwards 1513–28
Coll. 27 Jan. 1513 (*Reg. Mayew* p. 281). Conf. by bp. Booth 16 Jan. 1517 (*Reg. Booth* p. 17). Instal. 20 March (HCA 7031/1 fo. 3r). Preb. of Hunderton 1528. Biog. ref.: *BRUO 1500–40* p. 676.

M. Gamaliel Clifton DCnL 1528–9

Coll. 14 Apr. 1528 (*Reg. Booth* p. 341). Instal. in person 15 July (HCA 7031/1 fo. 44v). Preb. Colwall 1529. Also dean. Biog. ref.: *BRUC* p. 141.

M. Hugh Charnock 1529–51

Coll. 16 May 1529 (*Reg. Booth* p. 343). Instal. by proxy 17 May and again in person 20 May (HCA 7031/1 fo. 46v). D. by 24 Apr. 1551 (HRO, AL 19/14 fo. 84v); perhaps d. 1550 O.S. (*Survey of Cath.* I 597). Biog. ref.: *BRUO 1500–40* p. 112.

PREBENDARIES OF PRESTON

The endowment of this preb. was land in the hamlet of Preston in the parish of Withington, Herefs., which was valued at £8 in 1291, 12m in 1294 and £10 7s 4½d in 1535 (*Survey of Cath.* I 591; *Taxatio* p. 169a; *Reg. Swinfield* p. 305; *Valor* III 11).

M. Roger of Canterbury 1299–1303

Coll. 12 Nov. 1299 (*Reg. Swinfield* p. 531). Res. by 17 May 1303 to become preb. of Wellington. Also treas., archdcn. of Shropshire and preb. of Hinton.

M. William of Kingscote DCnL 1303–11

Coll. 17 May 1303 (*Reg. Swinfield* p. 531). D. by 18 Apr. 1311 (*ibid.* p. 540). Also preb. of Pratum Minus. Biog. ref.: *BRUO* II 1074.

William de Wyke 1311–20

Coll. 18 Apr. 1311 (*Reg. Swinfield* p. 540). Preb. of Episcopi 1320.

Thomas Talbot 1320–62

Coll. 17 Dec. 1320 (*Reg. Orleton* p. 386). Occ. as can. until 25 March × 23 June 1362 (HCA R439) and probably until d. by 23 May 1362 (*Reg. L. Charlton* p. 66).

M. William Winterton BCnL ?1362–86?

Expect. 31 May 1353 (*CPL* III 480). Occ. as can. from 25 March × 23 June 1362 (HCA R439) and this preb. 18 Nov. 1366 (Cant., *Reg. Langham* p. 40). Last occ. as can. 29 Sept. × 31 Dec. 1386 (HCA R451). Biog. ref.: *BRUC* pp. 642–3.

M. Edmund Ryall 1387–1428

Estate ratif. 9 Dec. 1387 (*CPR 1385–9* p. 376). D. 7 Apr. 1428 (*Survey of Cath.* I 592; *Reg. Spofford* p. 354). Biog. ref.: *BRUO* II 1614.

Nicholas Lyney 1428–9

Coll. 8 Apr. 1428 (*Reg. Spofford* p. 354). D. by 5 Jan 1429 (HCA 1795).

Henry Newton 1429–39

Coll. 28 Jan. 1429 (*Reg. Spofford* p. 355). D. by 26 Oct. 1439 (*ibid.* p. 362). Also preb. of Moreton Parva.

M. Robert Jordan 1439–55/6?

Coll. 26 Oct. 1439 (*Reg. Spofford* p. 362). Probably until 29 Sept. 1455 × 28 Sept. 1456 when Robert Geffrey first occ. as can. (HCA R493). Preb. of Bartonsham by 1462.

M. Robert Geffrey ?1455/6–67

Occ. as can. 29 Sept. 1455 × 28 Sept. 1456 (HCA R493) and this preb. 14 June 1462 (*Reg. Stanbury* p. 75). Preb. of Inkberrow 1467. Also chanc., treas. and archdcn. of Hereford and Shropshire. Biog. ref.: *BRUO* II 753–4.

M. Thomas St Just DMus 1467

Coll. 5 Jan. 1467 (*Reg. Stanbury* p. 183). D. by 22 Sept. (*ibid.* p. 184). Biog. ref.: *BRUC* p. 503.

Geoffrey Castelle 1467–8

Coll. 22 Sept. 1467 (*Reg. Stanbury* p. 184). Res. 29 Apr. 1468 and d. by 8 June (*ibid.* p. 185; *Registrum Thome Bourgchier, Cantuariensis Archepiscopi, AD 1454–86*, ed. F. R. H. DuBoulay (Canterbury and York Soc., liv, 1957) p. 293).

M. Robert Isham BCL 1468–86

Coll. 29 Apr. 1468 (*Reg. Stanbury* p. 185). Res. by 26 March 1486 (*Reg. Myllyng* p. 195). Biog. ref.: *BRUO* II 1006.

Thomas Isham 1486–?

Coll. 26 March 1486 (*Reg. Myllyng* p. 195). Occ. as can. 29 Sept. 1487 × 28 Sept. 1488 (HCA R525).

M. John Blythe ?–1512

Res. this preb. by 23 Oct. 1512 to become preb. of Wellington (*Reg. Mayew* p. 280).

M. Miles Ragon 1512–30/1

Coll. 23 Oct. 1512 (*Reg. Mayew* p. 280). Instal. 27 Nov. (HCA 7031/1 fo. 2r). D. as preb. 30 Sept. 1530 × 3 Jan. 1531 (HCA 7031/1 fo. 1; *Reg. Booth* p. 345). Also preb. of Moreton Parva.

M. John Gorle MA 1531–52

Coll. 3 Jan. 1531 (*Reg. Booth* p. 345, reading 'Yorke'). Instal. by proxy 5 July; instal. again in person s.d. (HCA 7031/1 fo. 67r). Occ. 1535 (*Valor* III 11). Preb. vac. by 18 May 1552 (Lamb., Reg. Cranmer fo. 133r). Biog. ref.: *BRUO* III 793.

PREBENDARIES OF PUTSON MAJOR

The endowment of this preb., sometimes called Vowchurch, was a carucate of land, rents and perquisites in the parish of St Martin's, Hereford, small commons and a portion of the ch. of Vowchurch, which was valued at £4 9s 8d in 1291, excluding the portion of the Vowchurch (*Fasti Hereford 1066–1300* p. 57; *Survey of Cath.* I 598, *Taxatio* p. 169b). The preb. of *Fowechurche* was valued at 18m in 1294 and

Putson Major at £10 13s 4½d in 1535, which included an annual portion of £7 from the ch. of Vowchurch (*Reg. Swinfield* p. 305; *Valor* III 9).

M. John de Swinfield 1287–1311?
Coll. 29 Jan. 1287 to preb. Vowchurch, a portion of Vowchurch was attached to this preb. (*Reg. Swinfield* p. 526; *Hereford Fasti 1066–1300* p. 58). Last occ. as can. 1 Jan. × 25 March 1311 (HCA R397). Also prec. Biog. ref.: A. B. Emden, 'Additions and corrections to *A Biographical Register of the University of Oxford to 1500* no. 2', *Bodleian Library Record*, vii (1964) 160.

M. Michael de Berham 1310–12
Coll. 24 Nov. 1310 and 18 Sept. 1311, suggesting perhaps that Knovile held both Putson prebs. (*Reg. Swinfield* p. 540). Exch. 22 March 1312, by which Hamo of Sandwich left Moreton and Whaddon and obtained preb. of Putson Major; Michael Berham left Putson Major and obtained preb. of Woolhope; John Winchelsea left Woolhope and obtained preb. of Moreton and Whaddon (*Reg. Swinfield* p. 541). Also preb. of Gorwell and Overbury. Biog. ref.: *BRUO* III 2151.

Hamo of Sandwich 1312–19
By exch. March 1312. Depriv. 2 Feb. 1319 (*Reg. Orleton* pp. 102, 116–17). Also preb. of Moreton and Whaddon.

M. John Trillek ?1333–44
Occ. as can. 29 Sept. × 31 Dec. 1333 (HCA R419). Res. this preb. to become bp. of Hereford 1344 (*CPR 1343–5* p. 361). Also preb. of Wellington. Biog. ref.: *BRUO* III 1906; D. Lepine, 'Trillek, John (*c.*1308–60)', *ODNB* <http://www.oxforddnb.com/view/article/95146>.

William Edington 1344–5
John de Makelesfeld 1344
Royal gr. to Edington 28 March 1344 and 8 Oct. (*CPR 1343–5* pp. 254, 363). Royal gr. in error to Makelesfeld 14 Oct., revoked 28 Oct. (*ibid.* p. 361). Edington became bp. of Winchester 1345, prov. 9 Dec. 1345, cons. 13 May 1346 (J. Le Neve, *Fasti Ecclesiae Anglicanae 1300–1541*, iv: *Monastic Cathedrals*, comp. B. Jones (1963) p. 46). Biog. ref.: Edington, *BRUO* I 629–30; R. G. Davies, 'Edington, William (d. 1366)', *ODNB* <http://www.oxforddnb.com/view/article/8481>.

John Bateman or Vienna 1346–9
Prov. 14 Feb. 1346 of preb. about to be void by cons. of Edington (*CPL* III 201). Conf. 6 Aug. 1346, although Edington had obtained it uncanonically (*ibid.* 237; *CPP* p. 115). D. 29 May 1349 (Salisbury Cathedral Archives, Reg. Corfe fo. 29). Biog. ref.: *Hemingby's Register* pp. 246–8.

Peter de Wotton ?–1358
M. Richard de la Barre 1354–5
Prov. unnamed preb. to Wotton 9 Oct. 1344, still expect. 15 June 1346 (*CPP* pp. 79, 111). Royal gr. to Barre 7 July 1354 (*CPR 1354–8* p. 91). Gr. revoked 5

March 1355 and Wotton conf. as preb. (*ibid.* p. 188; *Reg. Trillek* p. 45; *CPP* p. 78). Further papal conf. of Wotton 22 Oct. 1356 (*L&G* p. 125). Exch. 19 July 1358 with Nicholas Newton for preb. of Trallwng in colleg. ch. of Abergwili, Carm. (*Reg. Trillek* p. 409). Barre also preb. of Withington Parva.

M. Nicholas Newton BCnL 1358–76?

By exch. July 1358. Last occ. 25 March × 23 June 1376 (HCA R442).

M. John Upton ?–1384

Exch. this preb. 3 June 1384 with Richard Thurban for Nuthanger portion in Kingsclere, Hants., and preb. of Cowpes in St Martin-le-Grand, London (*Reg. Gilbert* p. 124). Also preb. of Putson Minor. Biog. ref.: *BRUO* III 1933.

Richard Thurban 1384–?

By exch. June 1384. Preb. of Putson Minor by 1387. Also preb. of Warham and Withington Parva.

M. John Godmanston 1389–1401

Royal gr. 26 Sept. 1389 (*CPR 1388–92* p. 115) and occ. as can. 29 Sept. × 31 Dec. 1390 (HCA R454). Estate ratif. 8 Nov. 1399 (*CPR 1399–1401* p. 55). Probably to d. by 18 June 1401 (London, GL MS. Reg. 9351/3 fo. 191v). Also preb. of Moreton Parva, Norton and Withington Parva.

Richard Talbot 1401–17

Coll. 6 June 1401 (*Reg. Trefnant* p. 185). Res. by 10 Nov 1417 (*Reg. Lacy H* p. 113). Also prec. Biog. ref.: *BRUO* III 1845–6; E. Matthew, 'Talbot, Richard (d. 1449)', *ODNB* <http://www.oxforddnb.com/view/article/26939>.

William Cave 1417–19

Coll. 10 Nov. 1417 (*Reg. Lacy H* p. 113). Exch. 12 May 1419 with John Malton for ch. of Michelmersh, Hants. (*ibid.* p. 119).

John Malton 1419–23

By exch. May 1419. Exch. 10 Aug. 1423 with John Delabere for chaplaincy of St Radegund's in St Paul's, London (London GL, MS. 25513 fo. 91; *Reg. Spofford* p. 368).

John Delabere 1423–7

By exch. Aug. 1423. Res. by 16 Dec. 1427 (*Reg. Spofford* p. 354).

William Torkesey or Porlessy 1427–?

Coll. 16 Dec. 1427 (*Reg. Spofford* p. 354).

William Myll ?–1453

D. as preb. by 14 Jan. 1453 (*Reg. Boulers* p. 23).

M. Vincent Clement DTh 1453–75?

Coll. 14 Jan. 1453 (*Reg. Boulers* p. 23). Occ. 14 June 1462 and 29 Sept. 1467 × 28 Sept. 1468 (*Reg. Stanbury* p. 75; HCA R637c). Probably until d. by March 1475 (*BRUO* I 432). Biog. ref.: *BRUO* I 432–3.

M. John Sebrond ?–1496

Probably succeeded Clement but first occ. as can. from 29 Sept. 1478 × 28 Sept. 1479 (HCA R168). D. as preb 16 June × 12 July 1496 (TNA, PROB 11/10).

M. Owen Pole DCnL ?1496–1509

Occ. as can. from 1485–6 and this preb. probably from 1496 when also treas. D. as preb. 10 × 18 Dec. 1509 (TNA, PROB 11/16; *Reg. Mayew* p. 277). Also held unidentified preb. Biog. ref.: *BRUO* III 1491.

M. Edmund Froucetur DTh 1509–18

Coll. 18 Dec. 1509 (*Reg. Mayew* p. 277). Second mand. adm. May 1510 (*ibid.* pp. 96–7). Preb. of Colwall 1518. Also dean, treas. and preb. of Norton. Biog. ref.: *BRUO* II 732.

M. William Hulle MA 1518–43

Coll. n.d. (on or after 28 Oct.) 1518 (*Reg. Booth* p. 332). Instal. by proxy n.d. *c.*1518 (HCA 7031/1 fo. 16v; fo. torn). D. 9 × 13 Aug. 1543 (TNA, PROB 11/30; HRO, AL 19/14 fo. 54v). Also chanc. Biog. ref.: *BRUO 1500–40* p. 684.

PREBENDARIES OF PUTSON MINOR

The endowment of this preb. was four acres at Putson, in the parish of St Martin's, Hereford, a watermill and rents in Putson, Ludlow and Hereford, which was valued at £6 7s 2d in 1291, 5m in 1294 and £4 9s 10d in 1535 (*Survey of Cath.* I 599; *Taxatio* p. 169a; *Reg. Swinfield* p. 305; *Valor* III 9).

Nicholas de Knovile 1281–1311

Coll. to preb. lately held by Richard Stratford 11 Feb. 1281 (*Reg. Cantilupe* p. 268). D. as preb. by 18 Sept. 1311 (*Reg. Swinfield* p. 540).

M. Richard de Havering ?1311–41

Expect. 21 Nov. 1310 (*CPL* II 80). First occ. as prec. 29 Sept. × 31 Dec. 1311 (HCA R399). Estate ratif. as preb. 10 Dec. 1330 (*CPR 1330–4* p. 25). D. by 22 July 1341 (*CPL* II 551). Also prec. Biog. ref.: *BRUO* III 2181–2.

M. Giles de Stamford ?1341–67
Peter Grelino 1342

By coll.; prov. 22 July 1341 (*CPL* II 551). First occ. 1 Jan. × 24 March 1341 (HCA R426). Prov. of Havering's preb. to Grelino 13 Aug. 1342 (*CPL* III 77). Stamford exch. 18 Jan. 1367 with Henry Shipton for portion in Westbury, Salop. (*Reg. L. Charlton* p. 72). Stamford also prec.

M. Henry de Shipton 1367–?
By exch. Jan 1367. Also prec., treas. and archdcn. of Shropshire and preb. of Hunderton.

John Upton 1372
M. Nicholas Hereford 1375, 1376
M. Thomas Chaundos junior 1376–?
Upton prov. to preb. vac. by d. of Stamford 18 Apr. 1372 (*L&G* p. 463). Prov. to Hereford 22 Feb. 1375 who gained possession in 1376 but was ejected after litigation by Chaundos (*L&G* p. 496). Chaundos also preb. of Cublington; Hereford also chanc., treas. and preb. of Pratum Majus and Minus; Upton also preb. of Putson Major. Biog. ref.: Upton, *BRUO* III 1933; Hereford, *BRUO* II 913–15.

Richard Thurban 1387–99
Estate ratif. as preb. 10 Aug. 1387 (*CPR 1385–9* p. 349). Res. by 29 Oct. 1399 (*Reg. Trefnant* p. 183). Also preb. of Putson Major, Warham and Withington Parva.

M. John Trefnant or **ap Howell** BCL 1399–1400
Coll. 29 Oct. 1399 (*Reg. Trefnant* p. 183). Preb. of Withington Parva 1400.

M. Thomas Chaundos junior ?–1406
D. as preb. by 9 Sept. 1406 (*Reg. Mascall* p. 169).

M. John Desford DCnL 1406–19
Coll. 9 Sept. 1406 (*Reg. Mascall* p. 169). D. 15 × 28 Apr. 1419 (TNA, PROB 11/2B; *Reg. Lacy H* p. 115). Biog. ref.: *BRUO* I 574.

John Dunstavyle 1419–40
Coll. 28 Apr. 1419 (*Reg. Lacy H* p. 115). Res. by 28 May 1440 (*Reg. Spofford* p. 362).

William Drokyll or **Throckurll** 1440–?
Coll. 28 May 1440 (*Reg. Spofford* p. 362). Occ. 14 July 1463 and 29 Sept. 1467 × 28 Sept. 1468 (*Reg. Stanbury* p. 75; HCA R637c).

M. Richard Martyn BCnL 1474–8
Coll. 10 March 1474 (*Reg. Stanbury* p. 189). Preb. of Huntington 1478. Also archdcn. of Hereford and preb. of Moreton Magna and Pratum Minus. Biog. ref.: *BRUO* II 1236–7; J. Hughes, 'Martyn, Richard (d. 1483)', *ODNB* <http://www.oxforddnb.com/view/article/18236>.

M. John Hervey BA 1478–89?
Coll. Feb. 1478 (*Reg. Myllyng* p. 188). Held this preb. probably until he became prec. in 1489. Also dean.

M. John Nans DCn&CL ?–1490
First occ. as can. 29 Sept. 1486 × 28 Sept. 1487 (HCA R524). Res. this preb. by 2 Nov. 1490 to become preb. of Gorwell and Overbury. Biog. ref.: *BRUO* II 1336–7.

Christopher Litton 1490–1505?
Coll. 2 Nov. 1490 (*Reg. Myllyng* p. 198). D. 9 Oct. × 2 Dec. 1505, as preb.? (TNA, PROB 11/14).

M. John Prat BCn&CL ?–1513
Occ. as can. unidentified preb. 1501–2. D. this preb. by 16 June 1513 (*Reg. Mayew* p. 281). Biog. ref.: *BRUO* III 1514.

John Viall 1513–25
Coll. 16 June 1513 (*Reg. Mayew* p. 281). D. 26 June × 14 July 1525 (HCA 7031/1 fo. 36v; *Reg. Booth* p. 338). Also preb. of Piona Parva. Biog. ref.: *BRUO 1500–40* p. 706.

M. John Mason BMus 1525–48
Coll. 22 July 1525 (*Reg. Booth* p. 338). Instal. in person 23 July (HCA 7031/1 fo. 36v). D. by 2 Feb. 1548 (HRO, AL 19/14 fo. 74v). Biog. ref.: *BRUO 1500–40* p. 386.

PREBENDARIES OF WARHAM

The endowment of this preb. was a carucate of land at Warham in the parish of Breinton, Herefs., which was valued at £6 13s 4d in 1291, 100s in 1294 and £7 13s 4d in 1535 (*Survey of Cath.* I 601; *Taxatio* p. 168b; *Reg. Swinfield* p. 305; *Valor* III 12).

M. Richard of Hertford 1293–1303
Coll. 21 March 1293 (*Reg. Swinfield* p. 529). D. by 1 June 1303 (*ibid.* p. 535). Also archdcn. of Hereford.

M. Henry de Shorne 1303–38?
Coll. 1 June 1303 (*Reg. Swinfield* p. 535). Occ. as can. until 25 March × 23 June 1338 (HCA R423), though said to be d. by 31 March 1337 (HCA 768). Also archdcn. of Hereford. Biog. ref.: *BRUO* III 1696.

M. John Offord DCL 1344
Robert de Wodhull 1344–?
Royal gr. to Offord 28 Jan 1344 which met with opposition (*CPR 1343–5* pp. 191, 199). Royal gr. to Wodhull 5 March (*ibid.* p. 216). Biog. ref.: Offord, *BRUO* II 1391–2.

Richard Prophete ?–1349
Exch. this preb. 8 March 1349 with John Prophete for ch. of Cusop, Herefs. (*Reg. Trillek* p. 406).

John Prophete 1349
By exch. March 1349. Preb. of Norton 1349.

M. Humphrey Charlton MA ?–1371

'Umfredo' occ. as can. unidentified preb. 1345 and last occ. 1361 (HCA R 430–8). Exch. this preb. 31 March 1371 with Richard Thurban for wardenship of Bawtry hospital, Yorks. (*Reg. Courtenay* p. 13). Biog. ref.: *BRUO* I 390–1.

Richard Thurban 1371–6

By exch. March 1371. Exch. this preb. 28 Oct. 1376 with William David for Nuthanger portion in Kingsclere, Hants. (Winchester, *Reg. Wykeham* I 81). Also preb. of Putson Major and Minor and Withington Parva.

William David 1376–83

By exch. Oct. 1376. Occ. as can. until 24 June × 28 Sept. 1383 (HCA R447). D. 16 Oct. 1383 (*Reg. Gilbert* p. 58).

M. Thomas Forneys 1384
M. Thomas Clone 1383–7

Both Forneys and Clone claimed papal prov. Forneys had prov. and expect. of preb. and dig. by Urban VI (HCA 3194). Clone occ. as can. 29 Sept. × 31 Dec. 1383 (HCA R448). Dispute settled in Clone's favour by the official of Hereford 29? Feb. 1384 (HCA 3194). He exch. 16 Apr. 1387 with Nicholas Salesbury for ch. of Stratfield Say, Hants. (Winchester, *Reg. Wykeham Register* I 160). Forneys also preb. of Withington Parva.

Nicholas Salesbury 1387–?
Walter Brugge 1392

Salesbury preb. by exch. Apr. 1387. Occ. 25 March × 23 June 1387 and estate ratif. 10 June 1388 (HCA R451; *CPR 1385–9* p. 461). Royal gr. to Brugge 28 Dec. 1392 (*CPR 1391–6* p. 207). Salesbury's estate ratif. 16 March 1400 (*CPR 1399–1401* p. 137).

Laurence Allerthorpe 1401–6

Coll. 7 June 1401 (*Reg. Trefnant* p. 185). D. 21 July 1406 (*Survey of Cath.* I 601; *Reg. Mascall* p. 169).

M. Thomas Felde DCL 1406–7

Coll. 22 July 1406 (*Reg. Mascall* p. 169). Exch. 8 Nov. 1407 with John Prophete for preb. of Moreton Magna (*ibid.* p. 183). Also dean and preb. of Withington Parva. Biog. ref.: *BRUO* II 682–3.

M. John Prophete 1407

By exch. 8 Nov. 1407. Exch. 16 Nov. with Roger Hore for preb. of Piona Parva (*Reg. Mascall* p. 183). Also dean and preb. of Moreton Parva. Biog. ref.: *BRUO* III 1521–3; R. G. Davies, 'Prophete, John (*c*.1350–1416)', *ODNB* <http://www.oxforddnb.com/view/article/37868>.

M. Roger Hore 1407–18

By exch. Nov. 1407. D. by 9 June 1418 (*Reg. Lacy H* p. 114). Also preb. of Piona Parva.

M. John Cokworthy 1418–19
Coll. 9 June 1418 (*Reg. Lacy H* p. 114). Preb. of Church Withington 1419.

Robert Trysk 1419
Coll. 28 Apr. 1419 (*Reg. Lacy H* p. 115). D. by 16 Nov. (*ibid.* p. 116).

William Kinwolmarsh 1419–?
Coll. 16 Nov. 1419 (*Reg. Lacy H* p. 116). D. 5 Oct. 1421 × 15 Dec. 1422, as preb.? (Cant., *Reg. Chichele* II 236; J. Le Neve, *Fasti Ecclesiae Anglicanae 1300–1541*, v: *St Paul's*, comp. J. M. Horn (1964) p. 67). Biog. ref.: Cant., *Reg. Chichele* II 660.

M. John Blodwell DCnL ?–1441
Occ. as can. 1 March 1427 when gr. canonical house (*Reg. Spofford* p. 353). Res. preb. by 18 June 1441 (*ibid.* p. 363). Biog. ref.: *BRUO* I 203.

David Blodwell 1441–61
Coll. 18 June 1441 (*Reg. Spofford* p. 363). D. by 13 Aug. 1461 (*Reg. Stanbury* p. 177). Biog. ref.: *BRUC* p. 66.

M. Simon Tawre BCnL 1461–4
Coll. 13 Aug. 1461 (*Reg. Stanbury* p. 177). Preb. of Cublington 1464. Also chanc. Biog. ref.: *BRUO* III 1860.

M. John Baily BCL 1464–6
Coll. 22 Aug. 1464 (*Reg. Stanbury* p. 180). Preb. of Ewithington 1466. Also prec. and preb. of Episcopi. Biog. ref.: *BRUO* I 91.

M. John Grenewey BCL 1466–86
Coll. 3 Apr. 1466 (*Reg. Stanbury* p. 182). D. by 3 May 1486 (*Reg. Myllyng* p. 195). Also preb. of Pratum Majus.

Henry Edvin or **Yedvin** or **Meysey** 1486–92/3?
Occ. as can. unidentified preb. 14 Apr. 1480 (*Reg. Myllyng* p. 190). Coll. this preb. 3 May 1486 (*ibid.* p. 195). Last occ. as can. 29 Sept. 1492 × 28 Sept. 1493 (HCA R530).

Thomas Grete ?1498/9–1508
Occ. as can. 29 Sept. 1498 × 28 Sept. 1499 (HCA R537). D. as preb. by 19 Oct. 1508 (*Reg. Mayew* p. 276).

M. Henry Martin BCn&CL 1508
Coll. 19 Oct. 1508 (*Reg. Mayew* p. 276). Preb. of Gorwell and Overbury Dec. Also archdcn. of Hereford and Shropshire and preb. of Inkberrow, Norton and Withington Parva. Biog. ref.: *BRUO* II 1234.

M. Roger Brayne BCnL 1509–27
Coll. 18 Jan. 1509 (*Reg. Mayew* p. 276). Res. by 14 Oct. 1509, second coll. s.d. (*ibid.*). D. by 7 March 1527 (*Reg. Booth* p. 340). Also treas. and preb. of Pratum Majus. Biog. ref.: *BRUO* I 255–6.

M. Walter Mey BTh 1527–33
Coll. 7 March 1527 (*Reg. Booth* p. 340). Preb. of Episcopi 1533. Biog. ref.: *BRUO 1500–40* p. 392.

M. Thomas Booth BCn&CL 1533–40
Coll. 20 Sept. 1533 (*Reg. Booth* p. 347). Instal. 17 Oct (HCA 7031/1 fo. 72v). Lic. to treat with Edward Baskerville for pension 7 Sept. 1539 (*Reg. Booth* p. 384). Res. by 17 Feb. 1540 (*Reg. Booth* p. 384; HRO, CA.19/14 fo. 6v).

M. Edward Baskerville DTh 1540–67
Coll. 17 Feb. 1540 (HRO, CA.19/14 fo. 6v). Instal. 18 Feb. (HCA 7031/1 fo. 84v). D. 11 × 23 Jan. 1567 (TNA, PROB 11/49; HRO, AL 19/15 (Scory) fo. 11r). Biog. ref.: *BRUO 1500–40* pp. 29–30.

PREBENDARIES OF WELLINGTON

The endowment of this preb. was the rectory of Wellington, Herefs., which was valued at £16 13s 4d, and a further £2 13s 4d for a share of the tithes, in 1291, 30m in 1294 and £14 in 1535 (*Survey of Cath.* I 603; *Taxatio* pp. 172a, 158b; *Reg. Swinfield* p. 305; *Valor* III 10).

John of Bridgnorth or **Ponte** or **Bruge** ?1278–1303
Occ. as can. 1271 × 1274, 24 June × 28 Sept. 1274 and this preb. 9 Feb. 1278 (*Reg. Swinfield* p. 57; HCA 2316, R3). D. 5 Jan. × 17 May 1303 (*Reg. Swinfield* pp. 380, 534).

M. Roger of Canterbury 1303
Coll. 17 May 1303; d. by 1 June (*Reg. Swinfield* p. 534). Also treas., archdcn. of Shropshire and preb. of Hinton and Preston.

Nicholas of Reigate 1303–8
Coll. 1 June 1303 (*Reg. Swinfield* p. 534). D. by 6 Apr. 1308 (*ibid.* p. 538). Also treas.

John de Costone 1308–20
Occ. as can. 29 Sept. 1307 × 28 Sept. 1308, probably this preb. (HCA R392). Occ. this preb. 29. Sept 1318 (*CPR 1318–23* p. 101). Removal ordered by bp. 5 March 1320 (*Reg. Orleton* p. 127). Res. 5 Aug. (*ibid.* p. 137).

William de Ayremynne 1320–5

Coll. by 5 March 1320 (*Reg. Orleton* p. 127). Bp.'s mand. adm. 6 Aug. (*ibid.* pp. 137–8). Bp. of Norwich 1325, prov. 19 July, cons. 15 Sept., royal assent 9 Nov. 1326. Biog. ref.: M. C. Buck, 'Airmyn, William (d. 1336)', *ODNB* <http://www.oxforddnb.com/view/article/944>.

John Talbot ?–1327
Roger Braynton 1326

Coll. to Braynton *in commendam* 16 Nov. 1326 (*Reg. Orleton* p. 389). Ineffective as Talbot had res. this preb. by 26 Sept. 1327 (*ibid.*). Braynton secured preb. of Norton 1326. Also preb. of Hunderton.

M. John Trillek 1327
M. John Walwayn DCL 1327–30

Coll. to Trillek on a papal reservn. (*Reg. Orleton* p. 389). Trillek occ. as can. 29 Sept. × 31 Dec. 1327 (HCA R414). Royal gr. to Walwayn 25 Dec. 1327 depriving Trillek but bp. refused to adm. Walwayn and k. recovered his right to pres. to preb. Easter term 1328 (*CPR 1327–30* p. 195; *CPL* II 316; *Select Cases in the Court of King's Bench under Edward III*, v, ed. G. O. Sayles (Selden Soc., lxxvi, 1958) pp. 31–2). Walwayn d. 22 July × 5 Sept. 1330 (*CPL* III 319, 499). Trillek also preb. of Putson Major and bp. of Hereford; Walwayn also preb. of Bullinghope. Biog. ref.: Trillek, *BRUO* III 1906; D. Lepine, 'Trillek, John (c.1308–60)', *ODNB* <http://www.oxforddnb.com/view/article/95146>; Walwayn, *BRUO* III 2225.

M. Laurence de la Barre MA 1331–6

Prov. 17 Dec. 1331 (*CPL* II 360). Occ. as can. from 29 Sept. × 31 Dec. 1332 to 24 June × 28 Sept. 1336 (HCA R418–21). D. by 11 Oct. 1336 (*BRUO* I 555–6). Biog. ref.: *BRUO* I 555–6.

M. Lewis Charlton 1336–61

Coll. 25 Sept. 1336 (*Reg. T. Charlton* p. 80). Bp. of Hereford 1361, prov. 10 Sept. 1361, spirit. 3 Nov. Biog. ref.: *BRUO* I 391–2; W. J. Dohar 'Charlton, Lewis (d. 1369)', *ODNB* <http://www.oxforddnb.com/view/article/5166>.

Richard de Ravenser 1361–3

Royal gr. 13 Nov. 1361 (*CPR 1361–4* p. 103). Exch. 2 July 1363 with Nicholas Haukyn for preb. of Barnby in Howden colleg. ch., Yorks. (York, Borthwick Institute, Reg. 11 fo. 55v). Biog. ref.: McDermid, *Beverley Fasti* pp. 50–1; A. K. McHardy, 'Ravenser, Richard (d. 1386)', *ODNB* <http://www.oxforddnb.com/view/article/23173>.

Nicholas Haukyn 1363–9

By exch. July 1363. Res. by 28 July 1369 (*CPR 1367–70* p. 288).

M. Thomas de Lexham DCnL 1369–82

Royal gr. 28 July 1369 (*CPR 1367–70* p. 288; HCA 2253). Last occ. as can. 24 June × 28 Sept. 1382 (HCA R446). D. 31 Oct. 1382 × 4 May 1383 (*BRUC* p. 366). Biog. ref.: *BRUC* p. 366.

Robert Muskham 1382–4
M. Walter of Ramsbury 1384–1406
M. John Outheby BCL 1391

Expect. to Ramsbury 28 Jan. 1371 (*L&G* p. 431; *Reg. Gregoire XI* no. 8015) but Muskham occ. as can. 24 June × 28 Sept. 1382 and continues to 29 Sept. × 31 Dec. 1384 (HCA R446–9). Muskham excomm. by papal authority (Lamb., MS. 221 fo. 231r). Ramsbury occ. as can. 1 Jan. × 24 March 1384 and continuously until d. (HCA R448). Prov. to Outheby 14 March 1391 (*CPL* IV 418). Ramsbury d. as preb. by 17 Nov. 1406 (*Reg. Mascall* p. 169). Ramsbury also prec. Biog. ref.: Ramsbury, *BRUO* III 1544–5.

Henry Myle 1406–20

Coll. 17 Nov. 1406 (*Reg. Mascall* p. 169). D. by 21 Apr. 1420 (*Reg. Lacy H* p. 116). Also prec.

M. Walter London BCL 1420

Coll. 21 Apr. 1420 (*Reg. Lacy H* p. 116). Res. by 20 Sept. (*ibid.* p. 117). Biog. ref.: *BRUO* II 1158–9.

M. John Baysham BCnL 1420–34

Coll. 20 Sept. 1420 (*Reg. Lacy H* p. 117). Probably to d. 21 March × 23 Oct. 1434 (Cant., *Reg. Chichele* II 503–5). Also dean and preb. of Moreton and Whaddon and Withington Parva. Biog. ref.: *BRUO* I 135–6.

M. Richard Martin 1434–42

Coll. 13 June 1434 (*Reg. Spofford* p. 359). Exch. 27 Feb. 1442 with Thomas Lewesham for canonry and preb. in Exeter (*ibid.* p. 369; *Reg. Lacy Exeter* p. 270). Also preb. of Norton.

Thomas Lewesham 1442–61

By exch. Feb. 1442. Res. by 20 Nov. 1461 (*Reg. Stanbury* p. 177).

M. James Goldwell DCn&CL 1461–4

Coll. 20 Nov. 1461 (*Reg. Stanbury* p. 177). Exch. 7 Oct. 1464 with Walter Petewynne for preb. of Ferring in Chichester (*ibid.* p. 192). Also dean. Biog. ref.: *BRUO* II 783–6; R. C. E. Hayes, 'Goldwell, James (d. 1499)', *ODNB* <http://www.oxforddnb.com/view/article/10926>.

M. Walter Petewynne DTh 1464–8

By exch. Oct. 1464. Exch. 20 July 1468 with Thomas Downe for preb. of Episcopi (*Reg. Stanbury* p. 192). Biog. ref.: *BRUO* III 1475.

Thomas Downe 1468–89

By exch. July 1468. D. 26 March 1489 (*Reg. Myllyng* p. 197; *Survey of Cath.* I 540). Also prec. and preb. of Episcopi.

M. Ralph Hauyes BCnL 1489–1501/2

Held this preb. after Apr. 1489 (*Reg. Myllyng* p. 197). Occ. as can. 8 March 1494 and 29 Sept. 1497 × 28 Sept. 1498 (*CPL* XVI no. 282; HCA R530). D. as preb. 10 Apr. 1501 × 29 Oct 1502 (TNA, PROB 11/13). Also preb. of Eigne and Piona Parva.

Robert Castellensis or **Munceo** ?–1508

D. as preb. by 7 Oct. 1508 (*Reg. Mayew* p. 276). Biog. ref.: McDermid, *Beverley Fasti* pp. 43.

M. William Webbe MA 1508–12

Coll. 7 Oct. 1508 (*Reg. Mayew* p. 276). Preb. of Inkberrow 1512. Also archdcn. of Hereford and Shropshire and preb. of Gorwell and Overbury and Moreton Magna. Biog. ref.: *BRUO* III 2004.

M. Henry Martin BCn&CL 1512

Coll. 12 June 1512 (*Reg. Mayew* p. 280). Instal. 26 July (HCA 7031/1 fo.1r). Preb. of Inkberrow Oct. 1512. Also archdcn. of Hereford and Shropshire and preb. of Gorwell and Overbury, Norton and Warham. Biog. ref.: *BRUO* II 1234.

M. John Blythe 1512–58

Coll. 15 Nov. 1512 (HRO, AL 19/12 fo. 70). Instal. by proxy 23 Nov. (HCA 7031/1 fo. 2). D. by 20 Sept. 1558 (HCA 7031/1 fo. 152). Also preb. of Preston.

PREBENDARIES OF WITHINGTON PARVA

The endowment of this preb. was land in the parish of Withington, Herefs., which was valued at £3 10s in 1291, 60s in 1294 and £3 4½d in 1535 (*Survey of Cath.* I 605; *Taxatio* p. 169a; *Reg. Swinfield* p. 305; *Valor* III 10).

Nicholas de Genville 1287–1301

Royal request for canonry 25 Feb. 1283 refused because under age (*Reg. Swinfield* pp. 1–2). Coll. 28 Jan. 1287 (*ibid.* p. 526). Res. by 16 Apr. 1301 from 'a preb. in the cath.' (*ibid.* p. 533).

Amadeus FitzPeter de Marnay 1301–?

Coll. 16 Apr. 1301 to preb. vac. by Nicholas de Genville (*Reg. Swinfield* p. 533).

Richard Passmer ?1339–50

Expect. 1 July 1331 (*CPL* II 343). Occ. as can. 25 March × 23 June 1339 (HCA R424). D. as preb. by 20 Apr. 1350 (*Reg. Trillek* p. 383).

M. William de Herewynton DCL 1350
M. Adam de Houghton DCL ?1352–61

John Benelard or **de Bono Villario** ?–1350
John Gros 1350–1
M. Roger Herlaston BCL 1351
Coll. to Herewynton 20 Apr. 1350 who also received papal conf. 9 Sept. 1350 (*Reg. Trillek* p. 383; *CPP* p. 204). Expect. to Houghton 1 Feb. 1347, still expect. 22 June 1349, but occ. as can. by 1352 (*CPP* p. 106; *CPL* III 238, 336; *Reg. Trillek* pp. 181, 225) and held preb. until bp. of St Davids 1361. Benelard occ. as can. of unidentified preb., perhaps this one, from 29 Sept. 1312 × 28 Sept. 1313 until 24 June × 28 Sept. 1329 (HCA R399–407), and d. as preb., allegedly, by 6 Oct. 1350, and royal gr. to Gros s.d. (*CPR 1350–4* p. 15). Gros never in full possession and the preb. continued to be held by Houghton (*L&G* p. 110). Gros res. by 23 Nov. 1351 (*CPP* p. 223). Prov. to Herlaston 23 Nov. 1351 but he was also ousted by Houghton (*ibid.*; *L&G* p. 110). Herlaston occ. as can. with unidentified preb. 5 Nov. 1355 (HCA 2839). Herewynton also preb. of Moreton and Whaddon. Biog. ref.: Herewynton, *BRUO* II 921; Houghton, *BRUO* II 972–3; Gros, *BRUO* II 830.

John Caven or **Carrewe** 1361
M. Richard de la Barre ?–1386
Expect. to Barre 28 Sept. 1361 (*CPP* p. 377). Prov. of Houghton's preb. to Caven 30 Oct. 1361 (*L&G* p. 162). Probably never in possession. Barre occ. 18 Nov. 1366 (*Reg. Langham* p. 42). Occ. as can. regularly from 29 Sept. × 31 Dec. 1372 until 1 Jan. × 24 March 1386 (HCA R 440–50). D. 16 Oct. 1386 (Havergal, *Mon. Inscr. Heref.* p. 29). Barre also gr. preb. of Putson Major.

Thomas Forneys 1386
By prov., adm. 16 Oct. 1386 (HCA 3195). Exch. 10 Dec. with John Godmanston for chap. of Reynalton, Pemb. (*Reg. Gilbert* p. 125). Also claimed preb. of Warham.

M. John Godmanston 1386–9
By exch. Dec. 1386. Coll. 8 Feb. 1387 (HCA 3195). Instal. 15 Feb. (HCA 2473). Estate ratif. 12 Aug. (*CPR 1385–9* p. 361). Royal gr. 25 July 1389 (*CPR 1388–92* p. 92). Preb. of Putson Major Sept. 1389. Also preb. of Moreton Parva and Norton.

Richard Thurban 1389
Royal gr. 26 Sept. 1389 (*CPR 1388–92* p. 113). Ineffective as already preb. of Putson Minor. Also preb. of Putson Major and Warham.

M. John Trefnant or **ap Howell** BCL ?1400–4
Estate ratif. 12 Feb. 1400 (*CPR 1399–1401* p. 137). Exch. 6 Jan. 1404 with Thomas Felde for preb. of Meliden in St Asaph (*Reg. Trefnant* p. 191). Also preb. of Putson Minor.

M. Thomas Felde DCL 1404–6
By exch. Jan. 1404. Preb. of Warham 1406. Also dean and preb. of Moreton Magna. Biog. ref.: *BRUO* II 682–3.

M. John Baysham BCnL 1406–7

Coll. 22 July 1406 (*Reg. Mascall* p. 169). Preb. of Moreton and Whaddon 1407. Also dean and preb. of Wellington. Biog. ref.: *BRUO* II 135–6.

M. John Loveney 1407–22

Coll. 25 Aug. 1407 (*Reg. Mascall* p. 172). Exch. 21 July 1422 with John Merbury for ch. of Kedington, Suff.(?) (*Reg. Spofford* p. 368). Also archdcn. of Hereford and Shropshire.

M. John Merbury 1422–?

By exch. July 1422. Occ. as archdcn. of Shropshire 14 Dec. 1434 and also preb.? (*Reg. Spofford* p. 54).

M. Robert Haliday or **Unert** ?–1429

D. as preb. by 16 Nov. 1429 (*Reg. Spofford* p. 356).

M. John Barowe BCnL 1429–62

Coll. 16 Nov. 1429 (*Reg. Spofford* p. 356). D. 6 Apr. 1462 (*Reg. Stanbury* p. 74). Also dean. Biog. ref.: *BRUO* I 116.

Hugh Ragon 1462–3

Coll. 13 Apr. 1462 (*Reg. Stanbury* p. 178). Preb. of Gorwell and Overbury 1463. Also preb. of Pratum Majus and unidentified preb.

John ap Richard 1463–82

Coll. 21 Dec. 1463 (*Reg. Stanbury* p. 179). D. by 17 Feb. 1482 (*Reg. Myllyng* p. 192). Also treas. and elected dean.

M. John Cole MA ?1504/5–15

M. Cole occ. as can. 29 Sept. 1504 × 28 Sept. 1505 (HCA R547). Res. this preb. by 9 May 1515 (*Reg. Mayew* p. 283). Biog. ref.: *BRUO* I 461.

M. John Elton or **Baker** BCn&CL 1515–47

Coll. 9 May 1515 (*Reg. Mayew* p. 283). D. 17 Apr. × 22 Aug. 1547 (TNA, PROB 11/31; Wiltshire and Swindon RO, Salisbury Diocesan Records, D1/2/16 fo. 36v; *Chapter Acts of the Cathedral Church of St Mary of Lincoln, A.D. 1547–59*, ed. R. E. G. Cole (Lincoln Record Soc., xv, 1920) p. 3). Biog. ref.: *BRUC* p. 210.

CANONS WITH UNIDENTIFIED PREBENDS

NB. There is some uncertainty about possession of an unidentified preb. when the only evidence is from the papal regs. or letters where the distinction between being gr. a prov. and gaining possession is not always clearly made. These are marked with an asterisk.

Richard Bartonsham ?1302/3–5/6?

Occ. 29 Sept. 1302 × 28 Sept. 1303 to 29 Sept. 1305 × 28 Sept. 1306 (HCA R390).

Simon Leversam occ. 1303/4
Occ. 29 Sept. 1303 × 28 Sept. 1304 (HCA R390).

M. Adam of Cirencester ?1306/7–11?
Occ. 29 Sept. 1306 × 28 Sept. 1307 (HCA R391). Last occ. 29 Sept. × 31 Dec. 1311 (HCA R399). Biog. ref.: *BRUO* I 532.

M. John de Solerio* ?1309–21?
Occ. 25 Dec. 1309 (*Reg. Clement V* no. 5256). Last occ. 25 May 1321 (*Reg. Jean XXII* no. 14282). Biog. ref.: *BRUO* III 1726.

William de Bliburgo or **Blythburgh** ?1310–13
Occ. 17 March 1310 (HCA 2595). D. as can. by 7 Feb. 1313 (*Reg. Swinfield* p. 483).

M. Adam Carbonel ?1310–38?
Occ. 29 Sept. × 31 Dec. 1310 (HCA R396). Said to have held canonry for five months 7 Nov. 1311 when gr. dispensation for illegitimacy (*Reg. Clement V* no. 7387). Last occ. 29 Sept. × 31 Dec. 1338 (HCA R424).

M. Adam Orleton DCnL ?1311–17
Occ. 1 Jan. × 24 March 1311 and 28 March 1317 (HCA R397; *CPL* II 141). Bp. of Hereford 1317. Biog. ref.: *BRUO* II 1402–4; R. M. Haines, 'Orleton, Adam (*c.*1275–1345)', *ODNB* <http://www.oxforddnb.com/view/article/96>.

John de Cosironne* occ. 1312
Occ. 7 July 1312 (*Reg. Clement V* no. 8556).

Richard Divite or **Divire** or **Divine*** occ. 1317, 1318
Occ. 10 July 1317 (*Lettres Jean XXII* no. 4382) and 10 July 1318 (*ibid.* no. 7725).

M. John de Clara* occ. 1317
Occ. 9 July 1317 (*CPL* II 154).

M. Alan Aslackby or **Haselachy** occ. 1319, 1321
Occ. 29 Sept. × 31 Dec. 1319 and 1 Jan. × 24 March 1321 (HCA R408–9).

M. Thomas Orleton ?1319–20?
Occ. 29 Sept. × 31 Dec. 1319 until 29 Sept. × 31 Dec. 1320 (HCA R408–9). Chanc. 1322.

M. Thomas Chaundos senior occ. 1324, 1330
Preb. Eigne 1317–? Occ. another preb. 28 Aug. 1324 and 1 June 1330 (HCA 2885; *CPR 1327–30* p. 530). Archdcn. Hereford 1318–32. Also preb. of Eigne. D. by 3 Jan. 1333 (*Calendar of Inquisitions Post Mortem* VII no. 492).

M. Adam Murimuth DCL ?1327–43?

Preb. Bullinghope 1320–1. Occ. frequently 1323–43: 15 Sept. 1323, 2 Nov. 1325, 29 Sept. × 31 Dec. 1327 to 29 Sept. × 31 Dec. 1335 and 1 Nov. 1343 (*CPL* II 239, 247; HCA R414–18; HCA R133). Biog. ref.: *BRUO* II 1329–30; W. R. Childs, 'Murimuth, Adam (1274/5–1347)', *ODNB* <http://www.oxforddnb.com/view/article/19567>.

J[ohn?] de Barton occ. 1330, 1331

Occ. 25 March × 23 June 1330 and 1 Jan. × 24 March 1331 (HCA R416–17). Probably archdcn. of Hereford in 1333. Occ. 29 Sept. 1335 when gr. canonical house (*Reg. T. Charlton* p. 79).

Hicherus occ. 1331

Occ. 24 June × 28 Sept. 1331 (HCA R417).

M. Nicholas Stockton occ. 1333

Prov. 3 Feb. 1330 (*CPL* II 305). Occ. 1 Jan. × 24 March 1333 (HCA R418). D. May 1341, as can.? (*BRUO* III 1786). Biog. ref.: *BRUO* III 1786.

M. Humphrey Charlton MA ?1345–?

'Umfredo' occ. 25 March × 23 June 1345 (HCA R430). Last occ. 1 Jan. × 24 March 1361 (HCA R439). Preb. Warham 1371, probably from 1349. Biog. ref.: *BRUO* I 390–1.

M. Richard de Welles* BCL occ. 1347

Prov. 29 March 1344, occ. as can. 21 Apr. 1347 (*CPP* p. 47; *CPL* III 228).

A. Glouc[ester?] occ. 1353

Occ. 25 March × 23 June 1353 (HCA R432).

M. Roger Herlaston BCL occ. 1355

Occ. 5 Nov 1355 (HCA 2839). Claimed preb. of Withington Parva.

Simon Burley ?1380–?

Occ. 24 June × 28 Sept. 1380 until 24 June × 28 Sept. 1387 (HCA R445–51). Preb. Norton 1390.

Samuel occ. 1382

Occ. 1 Jan. × 24 March 1382 to 29 Sept. × 31 Dec. 1382 (HCA R446–7).

William Hertewyke ?1382–91?

Occ. 25 March × 23 June 1382 until 24 June × 28 Sept. 1391 (HCA R446–54).

Robert Marescall or **Marshall** ?1389–91?

Occ. from 29 Sept. × 31 Dec. 1389 until 25 March × 23 June 1391 and 30 June 1391 (HCA 2975, R453–4).

John Russhale or **Russell** occ. 1392, 1398
Occ. 29 Sept. × 31 Dec. 1392, 7 Nov. 1393 and 29 June 1398 (HCA R455; *Reg. Trefnant* p. 57; HCA R630).

Nichol occ. 1394
Occ. 2 Oct. 1394 (HCA R630).

M. John Dylew or **Dellow** BCn&CL ?1435/6–46/7?
Occ. as can. 29 Sept. 1435 × 28 Sept. 1436 to 29 Sept. 1446 × 28 Sept. 1447 (HCA R481–5). Preb. Episcopi from 29 Sept. 1448 × 28 Sept. 1449. Also chanc. Biog. ref.: *BRUO* I 566–7.

R[obert?] Ascu[Aiscough?] occ. 1438/9
Occ. 29 Sept. 1438 × 28 Sept. 1439 (HCA R476).

R. Alkot occ. 1443/4
Occ. 29 Sept. 1443 × 28 Sept. 1444 (HCA R483).

Hugh Ragon ?1471/2–1501/2?
Preb. Pratum Majus 1460–2, Withington Parva 1462–3 and Gorwell and Overbury 1463–71/2. Occ. 29 Sept. 1471 × 28 Sept. 1472 until 29 Sept. 1501 × 28 Sept. 1501 (HCA R508–41).

M. Owen Lloyd DCL ?–1478
D. as can. by 30 Oct. 1478 (*BRUO* II 1153–4). Biog. ref.: *BRUO* II 1153–4.

M. R[alph?] Barton ?1478/9–92/3?
Occ. 29 Sept. 1478 × 28 Sept. 1479 to 29 Sept. 1492 × 28 Sept. 1493 (HCA R168–75). Preb. Pratum Majus 1467–76.

Henry Edvin or **Yedvin** or **Meysey** ?1480–85/6?
Occ. 1480 and from 29 Sept. 1480 × 28 Sept. 1481 until 29 Sept. 1485 × 28 Sept. 1486 (*Reg. Myllyng* p. 190; HCA R517–22). Preb. Warham 1486.

M. Robert Kent DTh ?1486/7–?
Occ. 29 Sept. 1486 × 28 Sept. 1487 (HCA R524). Preb. Episcopi 1504 × 1516. Also prec. Biog. ref.: *BRUO* II 1037.

M. John Taylor occ. 1479/80, 1480/1
Occ. 29 Sept. 1479 × 28 Sept. 1480 and 29 Sept. 1480 × 28 Sept. 1481 (HCA R516–17). D. 23 Dec. 1492, as can.? (*BRUO* III 1850–1). Biog. ref.: *BRUO* III 1850–1?

M. Owen Pole DCnL ?1485/6–?
Occ. from 29 Sept. 1485 × 28 Sept. 1486 (HCA R522). Treas. 1496 and probably preb. Putson Major 1496. Biog. ref.: *BRUO* III 1491.

M. John Benet ?1491/2–7/8

Occ. 29 Sept. 1491 × 28 Sept. 1492 (HCA R529). Last occ. 29 Sept. 1497 × 28 Sept. 1498 (HCA R536). D. 6 Dec. 1497 × 9 June 1498 (*BRUC* p. 54).

M. John Rokke ?1495/6–1501/2?

Occ. 29 Sept. 1495 × 28 Sept. 1496 (HCA R532). Last occ. 29 Sept. 1501 × 28 Sept. 1502 (HCA R541). Biog. ref.: *BRUO* III 1585?

M. Richard Draper ?1497/8–99

Occ. 29 Sept. 1497 × 28 Sept. 1498 (HCA R536). D. as can. 24 June × Aug. 1499 (TNA, PROB 11/12; *BRUO* III 2171). Biog. ref.: *BRUO* III 2171.

M. Warde occ. 1497/8

Occ. 29 Sept. 1497 × 28 Sept. 1498 (HCA R536).

M. John Argentine MD ?1498/9–1500/1?

Occ. 29 Sept. 1498 × 28 Sept. 1499 until 29 Sept. 1500 × 28 Sept. 1501 (HCA R537–40). D. 2 Feb. 1508, as preb.? (*BRUC* pp. 15–16). Biog. ref.: *BRUC* pp. 15–16.

M. Rede occ. 1499/1500

Occ. 29 Sept. 1499 × 28 Sept. 1500 (HCA R538).

William Bruer ?1501/2–3/4?

Occ. 29 Sept. 1501 × 1502 until 29 Sept. 1503 × 28 Sept. 1504 (HCA R541–4).

M. Christopher Plummer BCL occ. 1500/1, 1501/2

Occ. 29 Sept. 1500 × 28 Sept. 1501 and 29 Sept. 1501 × 28 Sept. 1502 (HCA R540–1). Attainted and sent to the Tower 27 May 1534, as can.? (*BRUO* III 1487). Biog. ref.: *BRUO* III 1487.

M. John Prat BCn&CL ?1501/2–?

Occ. from 29 Sept. 1501 × 28 Sept 1502 until 29 Sept. 1507 × 28 Sept. 1508 (HCA R541–7). Preb. Putson Major 1513. Biog. ref.: *BRUO* III 1514.

M. T. Solferd occ. 1503/4

Occ. 29 Sept. 1503 × 28 Sept. 1504 (HCA R544).

INEFFECTIVE PROVISIONS AND EXPECTATIONS TO PREBENDS AND DIGNITIES

John de Bruneshope 1317

Expect. 19 March 1317 (*Lettres Jean XXII* no. 3219).

John son of Palyologi Zachariae 1317

Expect. 15 Apr. 1317 (*Lettres Jean XXII* no. 3441).

William de Boudon 1323
Expect. preb. 4 Sept. 1323, still expect. 24 June 1325 (*Lettres Jean XXII* no. 18040; *CPL* II 244).

William de Thunneyk 1327
Prov. to canonry 10 Oct. 1327 (*Lettres Jean XXII* no. 30045).

Robert de Fileby 1331
Expect. preb. 13 March 1331 and 21 Nov. 1331 (*Lettres Jean XXII* nos. 53064, 55744).

Ralph Horncastle 1331
Expect. 10 Nov. 1331, still expect. 18 June 1333 (*Lettres Jean XXII* nos. 55620, 60569).

John Travers 1332
Expect. 3 Aug. 1332 (*Lettres Jean XXII* no. 57957).

M. Walter Buxton 1333
Expect. 22 Sept. 1333 (*Lettres Jean XXII* no. 61494). Biog. ref.: *BRUC* p. 113.

John de Clifford 1343
Reservn. canonry and preb. 17 July 1343, still expect. 5 Aug. 1345 (*CPP* pp. 66, 103).

Richard de Aston 1343
Prov. unnamed preb. 19 Sept. 1343, still expect. 9 March 1353 (*CPL* III 133; *CPP* p. 239).

Baldwin Talbot 1343
Prov. to deanery and reservn. unnamed preb. 12 Nov. 1343 (*CPP* p. 29).

Robert Wellesbourne 1347
Expect. 30 June 1347 (*CPL* III 244; HCA 3213).

M. John Tresulian MA 1349
Prov. unnamed preb. 7 March 1349 (*CPP* p. 147). Biog. ref.: *BRUO* III 1897.

Reginald de Stanford 1349
Expect. 27 Apr. 1349 (*CPL* III 295).

Richard de Middleton 1349
Expect. 21 Aug. 1349 (*CPP* p. 174).

Vincent Coleman 1351
Reservn. unnamed preb. 8 Jan. 1351 (*CPL* III 417).

Henry Walton 1352
  Expect. 21 Feb. 1352 and again 25 Jan. 1353 (*CPP* pp. 225, 238).

John Sprot 1355
  Expect. 8 Feb. 1355 (*CPP* p. 278).

Robert de Frome 1358
  Expect. 6 Sept. 1358 (*CPP* p. 333).

William Wynel of Wenlock 1360
  Expect. 20 Oct. 1360 (*CPP* p. 360).

Henry de Haydock 1361
  Expect. 25 June 1361 (*CPP* p. 372).

M. Thomas Atturton BCL 1362
  Expect. preb. 31 Dec. 1362 (*Lettres Urbain V* no. 7476). Biog. ref.: *BRUO* I 72–3.

Thomas Lutton or **Lynton** 1363
  Expect. preb. 31 Aug. 1363 and again 17 Feb. 1371 (*Lettres Urbain V* no. 4246; *L&G* p. 420; *Lettres Gregoire XI* no. 13935).

M. William Flaynburgh or **Beverley** BCL 1369
  Prov. to dig. 27 Jan. 1369 (*L&G* p. 357). Biog. ref.: *BRUC* p. 233.

John Blake 1371
  Expect. preb. 11 March 1371 (*L&G* p. 421; *Lettres Gregoire XI* no. 14031).

Robert Wentbrigge 1371
  Expect. preb. 27 March 1371 (*L&G* p. 425).

William Ives 1371
  Expect. preb. 22 June 1371 (*L&G* p. 426).

Philip Underhill 1371
  Expect. preb. 17 June and 22 June 1371 (*Lettres Gregoire XI* no. 14268; *L&G* p. 426).

Roger Stamford 1371
  Expect. preb. 23 July 1371 (*L&G* p. 435; *Lettres Gregoire XI* no. 14327).

John Brandferry 1371
  Expect. preb. 1371 (*L&G* p. 452).

Nicholas de Lichfield 1372
  Expect. preb. 29 Feb. 1372 (*L&G* p. 461).

James Venne 1372
  Expect. preb. 17 Aug. 1372 (*L&G* p. 468).

Index

Persons are indexed under their family names. Significant variant forms of family names are included. Archdeacons of Shropshire with no reference to a diocese are archdeacons of Shropshire in the diocese of Hereford rather than the dioceses of Coventry and Lichfield.